ENCYCLOPEDIA OF SCHOOL HUMOR

ENCYCLOPEDIA OF SCHOOL HUMOR
Icebreakers, Classics, Stories, Puns & Roasts for All Occasions

P. Susan Mamchak
and
Steven R. Mamchak

Parker Publishing Company, Inc.   West Nyack, New York

© © 1987 by

PARKER PUBLISHING COMPANY, INC.

West Nyack, N.Y.

Library of Congress Cataloging-in-Publication Data

Mamchak, P. Susan,
　　Encyclopedia of school humor.

　　Includes index.
　　1. Public Speaking—Handbooks, manuals, etc.
　　2. Education—Anecdotes, facetiae, satire, etc.
　　I. Mamchak, Steven R.　　II. Title.
　　PN4193.I5M28　1987　　　808.5′1　　　86-18734

ISBN 0-13-276346-X

Printed in the United States of America

It is with deep gratitude that we
dedicate this book to
Patricia Costanzo, M.D.,
who has given us ample reason for joy.

ACKNOWLEDGMENT

We gratefully acknowledge the many (literally, thousands of) people who, over the years, have been kind and gracious enough to share with us some precious moments of humor and laughter. Although their faces and names may have faded with time, the joy of their stories and anecdotes continues to enliven and enrich us. Our deepest thanks for all these contributions over the years. They have been instrumental in the development of this book.

HOW TO USE THIS BOOK EFFECTIVELY

Encyclopedia of School Humor is for all educators who are constantly on the lookout for new and effective "tools of the trade." The only difficulty in using humor in education is that we are, after all, front-line educators and not professional joke writers. Finding a specific story to enhance a specific situation or enliven a topic can often be difficult and frustrating. Much of the "humor" we hear everyday on television and in other media is either inappropriate or inconsistent with our image as professionals and educators—or else it's simply not funny. For this reason, we need a reference book where we can find the humor we need with the assurance that, while funny, it is also dignified and appropriate to our position as educators.

Encyclopedia of School Humor was written to meet that need. It is a collection of humorous, witty anecdotes and stories gathered over the years by and from educators like yourself. The stories illustrate effectively the broad range of situations and ideas peculiar to education, while highlighting the relationships of educators and students, parents and teachers, and professional colleagues to one another—all the interactions that are a vital part of our daily professional lives. In these stories, you will find material well-suited to a variety of formal and informal speaking occasions.

For example, do you want to . . .

. . . break through the formality of a meeting and talk about various points of view? Then see Part 1: Icebreakers.

. . . describe adult interactions with children? See Part 2: Stories That Make a Difference.

. . . "poke a little fun" at fairy tales, the school athletic program, or children's imaginations? Read Part 3: Classroom Classics.

. . . discuss students' misconceptions and perceptions? Take a look at Part 4: Blunders, Bloopers, and Puns.

. . . talk about school administrators in a variety of situations? Then browse through Part 5: It's the "Principal" of the Thing.

. . . reflect on children's honesty and frankness? See Part 6: Where Do the Teachers Sleep?

. . . cover such topics as pets, field trips, and homework? Then see Part 7: It's the Little Things That Count.

. . . establish rapport with parents by talking about family life and education? Read Part 8: Let's Keep It in the Family.

. . . roast a fellow teacher or administrator who's being honored? Take a look at Part 9: Well-Roasted.

. . . share humorous stories about the age-old struggle of raising children? See Part 10: Just Plain Funny.

All the material in this book has been audience-tested and proven effective in a variety of situations, ranging from Back-to-School Night to PTA meetings to faculty meetings to the classroom. Each story is preceded by a listing of the topics it covers and the audience for which it is most effective. Following almost every story is a brief note detailing specific suggestions for its most effective use and/or the best method for its delivery.

A special "Topic Finder" appears at the end of the book. This section cross references every story in the book, and allows you to find the story you need on the topic of your choice in a few seconds.

In a dramatic and memorable fashion, *Encyclopedia of School Humor* will help you establish rapport, sway an audience, prove your point, and—perhaps most important of all—teach. Its wide variety of humorous material directly related to today's educational scene, combined with its easy use and helpful suggestions, make *Encyclopedia of School Humor* a reference that will occupy a prominent position on your bookshelf. Enjoy using it today, and everyday—and use it with a smile!

P. Susan Mamchak

Steven R. Mamchak

CONTENTS

PART 5   IT'S THE "PRINCIPAL" OF THE THING **93**

PART 6   WHERE DO THE TEACHERS SLEEP? **117**

Part 1
Icebreakers

T he title of this section does not, of course, refer to those formidable ships that clear waterways of packed ice during winter months, but there is a great similarity. Those vessels break through the ice that has closed a river and establish a channel through which commerce can flow smoothly and unimpeded. So, too, the "icebreakers" in this section are designed to help the educator "break through" the formality that exists in many situations and establish a smooth channel of communication, a rapport, with the audience, whether that audience be in a classroom, at a formal meeting, or in a public speaking situation.

The foremost of educators have always known the value of humor. Indeed, the importance of laughing and having the world laugh with you was never more appreciated or more appropriate than in the educational setting. A carefully chosen piece of humor can set people at ease, make them well-disposed to what you have to say, help them remember a fact linked to the humor, and, in general, set a free and comfortable atmosphere in which learning and communication can flourish.

Not every story will fit every situation of course, but if you select one that gets at the point you are trying to make and if you match that story to your personality and style, you will have made an impression on your audience that no amount of lecturing, however thoroughly researched and documented, could hope to match.

And remember—if you enjoy yourself and have a good time, so will your audience. That's a fact!

1

TOPICS:
Quick thinking; inventiveness; questions and answers; famous people

AUDIENCE:
Suitable for all audiences from secondary students through adults

The story is told of Daniel Webster, the famous American patriot and historical figure, that he was frequently punished when he was a boy for coming to school with dirty hands.

One day as he was walking to school, he chanced to notice that his hands were particularly dirty, and it occurred to him that he was most likely in line for another punishment. Time was growing late, and, as there was no other means available, the young Webster proceeded to lick one hand as clean as circumstances would allow him to get it.

When he reached school, he carefully hid both hands behind his back. It was not long, however, before the schoolmaster approached him and inquired as to the cleanliness of his hands.

Young Daniel stood up and, from behind his back, produced the hand he had attempted to lick clean.

"Daniel," proclaimed the schoolmaster in a stern voice, "you should be ashamed of yourself. In fact, if you can find a dirtier hand than that in this entire school, I'll let you off without punishment!"

"Oh, thank you, sir!" proclaimed Daniel. And, taking his other hand from behind his back, he thrust it forward exclaiming, "Here it is!"

SPECIAL NOTE: This story provides a good start to a speech on problem solving or creative thinking. In a humorous manner, it brings out the necessity for finding innovative solutions and for using our own resources.

2

TOPICS:
Communications; the need for clear directions; misunderstanding

AUDIENCE:
Suitable for all audiences

I have a friend who really enjoys fishing. One day, he was out for a day's sport when his line became fouled, and apparently stuck, on something on the bottom. He was about to cut the line when it came loose, and he reeled it in to find that, by some quirk of chance, he had tangled his line around a rather large lobster.

As he was docking his boat at the end of the day, he noticed a friend standing on the pier.

He called to his friend and said, "Look, I really don't want this lobster. Why don't you take it home for supper?"

The friend agreed, put the lobster in a sack, and left.

My friend finished tying up his boat, and after he had cleaned up and changed his clothes, he decided to go out to a local diner for a bite to eat. He was just finishing his coffee when the door to the diner opened and in walked his friend, followed closely by the lobster, scuttling along clicking its claws noisily.

"Good grief!" exclaimed my friend, "I thought you were going to take him home for supper!"

"I did," his friend explained, "but he didn't seem to like anything I had at home, so I figured I'd take him here, and he could order what he wanted!"

SPECIAL NOTE: *The key to all these stories is personalization. In this one, for instance, you might assume the role of the fisherman and assign the role of the friend to a well-liked principal or teacher in the school or district. This would get even more laughter, and it is so obviously contrived that the audience will understand that it is all in fun.*

3

TOPICS:
Children; misconceptions; words and their meanings

AUDIENCE:
Adults, particularly parents

Uncle Joe and Aunt Mary had come over for dinner. and all through the meal six-year-old Tommy had been uncharacteristically silent. Indeed, he didn't say a word but spent the majority of the time gazing at Uncle Joe with a furious intensity.

Finally, the main part of the meal was finished and dessert was brought to the table. Despite the fact that the dessert was one of Tommy's favorites, the lad proceeded to lower his head and look as if somebody had just stolen his ice cream cone.

"Tommy," said Mother, "all night long you've done nothing but stare at Uncle Joe, and now you're all but pouting. Whatever is the matter?"

"Uncle Joe told a fib," said Tommy, raising his eyes.

"A fib? What do you mean?"

"Well," answered Tommy, "just before supper, when you and Daddy went out to the kitchen, I heard Uncle Joe tell Aunt Mary that if you served tuna casserole again, he was going to turn green.

"Well, you did, and he *didn't!*"

SPECIAL NOTE: This story gets a very big laugh from all adult audiences, but it seems to be the parents who laugh loudest of all. It also brings home the fact that we must understand that our children often cannot distinguish between denotative and connotative meanings. This can serve as a springboard to a discussion on meaningful communications.

4

TOPICS:
Optimism/pessimism; getting the right outlook

AUDIENCE:
Suitable for audiences that can grasp the concepts of optimism and pessimism; not for elementary students

NOTE:
What follows are several short entries on optimists, pessimists, and the difference between them.

> 'Twixt the optimist and the pessimist
> The difference is droll;
> The optimist sees the doughnut
> While the pessimist sees the hole!

* * *

An optimist is a man who sees the light that is not there, while the pessimist is the damn fool who is always trying to blow it out!

* * *

An optimist is a person who falls off the Empire State Building and as he passes the seventy-fifth floor, yells, "I'm still all right!"

* * *

A pessimist is a person who won't hang his stocking from the mantle, because he's convinced Santa Claus will steal it!

* * *

A pessimist says, "It can't be done!" and then smiles when, sure enough, everything crumbles just as he had predicted. An optimist, on the other hand, says, "I'll give it the best that I can!" and ruins the pessimist's good time.

SPECIAL NOTE: These are good lines to use when you want to "fire up" a group of people to do something, whether it be raising funds or writing a new curriculum. The descriptions hit home with every adult audience.

5

TOPICS:
Public speaking; after-dinner speeches; boredom

AUDIENCE:
Apt and suitable for any audience that has to listen to
a speech you are giving

NOTE:
Here are several lines to use at the start of any speech
that will help you establish almost instant rapport with
your audience. Try them; you'll find they work.

(When someone has given you a particularly flowery introduction . . .)
I want to thank Mrs. Jones for that marvelous introduction. All
I can say is that now I know how the toast feels after the butter *and*
the jam.

*　　*　　*

I'd like to start my speech this evening with a quote from the
Bible. I refer to the time when Daniel was thrown into the lion's den,
and he raised his voice and said, "Well, at least I won't have to listen
to the after-dinner speeches!"

*　　*　　*

You people do not know me
　Or what I am to say,
But my hope is when I'm finished,
　You'll like me anyway.
And since you've been so gracious,
　I'm going to be a sport
And give you all a present—
　I'm going to keep it short!

*　　*　　*

I once attended a high school graduation dinner at Morris High
School, where the speaker began, "Morris High School! M is for the

memories . . ." and continued for over an hour to extol the virtues of the school by talking about a word or phrase represented by each of the letters in the name. It was a particularly warm evening, and by the time he had finished, everyone was overheated and almost gasping for breath. At that point, I noticed the principal sitting with his head bowed. "Are you all right?" I asked. "I'm okay," he responded, "I was just praying." "Praying?" I questioned. "Yes," answered the principal, "I was thanking the Lord that our school wasn't named the Frederick T. Jackson Polytechnic Institute!"

*   *   *

SPECIAL NOTE: *Whenever you are the speaker, it is best to remember that a short, to-the-point speech is far more appreciated than any lengthy monologue, no matter how good it may be. The above lines are basically jokes on yourself, and these are always good ways of establishing rapport at the beginning of a speech.*

6

TOPICS:
Human nature; personal characteristics; frailties

AUDIENCE:
Suitable for most audiences

When I was teaching, I would often give my students a questionnaire to fill out in which I asked them to list their personal strengths and weaknesses. Later, we would enter into a discussion on how to capitalize on our strengths and improve in our areas of weakness.

One student, however, completely baffled me. Under "Personal Strengths" he wrote: "Very often I am thoughtful, kind, obedient, faithful, brave, and friendly. Also, I always use good grammar."

Then, under "Personal Weaknesses" he wrote: "Very often I am not thoughtful, not kind, not obedient, not faithful, not brave, and not friendly . . . and sometimes I don't use no good grammar at all!"

SPECIAL NOTE: We are certain that you see the possibilities for discussion that this story opens up, particularly from the approach that we all have good and bad qualities within us that have to be recognized. In the last line of the story, pause after the words "not friendly" and wait for the laugh. Then add the rest of the line for a "topper." It will get results.

7

TOPICS:
Hard work; concentrating effort; the academic life

AUDIENCE:
Suitable for all audiences

I have always made it a point to discuss their report cards with my children. When, one day, my son presented me with his report card by handing it to me with his head and eyes lowered, I knew it wasn't going to be good.

It wasn't. In fact, it was terrible. Out of six subjects, he had failed everything except English, and in that, he had somehow managed to get a "D."

"Well," I said, "this is going to take some explaining. Just how do you account for five failing grades?"

"I think I got it figured out, Dad," he answered. "I've just been spending too much time on English!"

SPECIAL NOTE: You can use this story to bring out the point that we must concentrate on all areas of the curriculum or of the child's learning experience, or on all sides of a problem, et cetera. Tell it with a twinkle in your eye and voice, and your audience will appreciate the message.

8

TOPICS:
Job pressures; difficulties of a profession; stress

AUDIENCE:
Suitable for all audiences, particularly educators

I have a friend who used to be the chairperson of the Math Department at a local high school. As we all know, that can be a pretty demanding position, and, gradually, his friends and colleagues noticed a decline in his health. It became evident that the gentleman was seriously ill, and hospital tests confirmed that he had acquired a serious ulcer problem.

"What can I do?" he asked friends. The doctor says relax, but the budgets are due, I have to get the book orders ready, and I must prepare a test for sixth period!"

"Bill," advised one teacher, "it's not worth your health. Why don't you take a medical leave and rest for awhile. Take a vacation. Learn to relax. It might do you a world of good."

My friend agreed and had no trouble getting his medical leave. The faculty and administration were a bit concerned, however, when they learned that for his "vacation" he had booked passage to a primitive country that was going through political unrest. Was this any way to "relax"?

Two months went by, and no one heard a word from him. Then, one day, a letter arrived at the school addressed to the faculty.

"Dear faculty," it read. "This is some place. Guerillas take pot shots at us from the trees; each night we have to check our beds for tarantulas; I was running out of money, so I have taken a job driving a nitroglycerin truck across the twisting mountain roads. And, guess what? Since I came here, my ulcers have cleared up!"

SPECIAL NOTE: For "department chairperson" you can substitute as you wish. With minor alterations, you might even make it be a parent. Adjusting this story to the discipline you are addressing will guarantee a laugh and, usually, a large round of applause.

9

TOPICS:
Adolescence; children and parents; teenage egotism

AUDIENCE:
Particularly suited to audiences of parents and/or educators

It was the great American humorist and author, Mark Twain, who remarked that when he was 16, he knew that his father was surely the most stupid man on the face of the earth, and that when he was 21, he was utterly amazed by how much the old man had learned in just five short years.

*   *   *

Adolescence is that period in children's lives when they steadfastly refuse to believe that in a few short years, they'll be as stupid as their parents.

*   *   *

Adolescence is that time in a parent's life when he is sorely tempted to ask his son or daughter how it felt to create the world.

*   *   *

Put the personality of a child into the body of an adult, furnish a need to be guided and a fierce desire to be independent, allow a need to be self-directing but leave out any idea of what direction to take, add an enormous amount of love but also the fear that it may not be accepted or returned, give physical and sexual powers without any knowledge or experience of how to use them—take these and place them in an adult society whose values and achievements are essentially incomprehensible and certainly unattainable, and whose concerns are seemingly misplaced and insincere. When you do all of this, you will have just begun to understand the problems of adolescence.

*   *   *

Over the course of a lifetime, a person usually goes from wide-eyed idealism to cautious conservatism. Parental difficulty in dealing with an adolescent usually arises from the fact that while adolescents are in the former stage, their parents are in the latter.

SPECIAL NOTE: *Adolescence is a difficult time in the life of every child and can produce some real problems. The lines above are reflective of both the humor and the depth of feeling associated with this turbulent period. They are particularly effective when used with groups of secondary educators and/or parents.*

10

TOPICS:
Inventiveness; discovery; looking for new solutions

AUDIENCE:
Suitable for all audiences

I have always believed in the validity of the "guided discovery" method. Indeed, I tried never to merely "give" my children the answer to a homework problem. Rather, I tried to point the way toward the answer and let them "discover" it for themselves.

That only backfired once. My daughter was studying pioneer life, and she came to me with a question.

"Daddy," she asked, "how did the pioneers start a fire?"

This was my chance, and true to my principles, I would not give her a direct answer. "I'll give you a hint," I said. "It has to do with two sticks."

Over the next few days, my daughter began to amass a sizable collection of sticks of all shapes and sizes. I smiled inwardly as she proceeded to experiment.

Finally, she came to me with the paper she had written for school. "When the pioneers wanted to start a fire," she wrote, "they went and got two sticks . . . and they made darn sure that one of them was a match!"

SPECIAL NOTE: This is another story that can effectively be used to introduce a new program or new procedures by emphasizing the need to experiment in order to come up with solutions that work and making certain that we have arrived at the RIGHT solution.

11

TOPICS:
Placing blame; perceptions of problems; interpersonal relations

AUDIENCE:
Effective when used with parents and/or educators

The question on the art test asked the student to draw a straight line. Young Mary's line was anything but straight.

"My goodness," said the art teacher, "this child must have a perceptual problem. Perhaps the child study team can do something with her."

"It isn't perceptual," reported the child study team. "Let's see if the school psychologist can tell us why Mary can't draw a straight line."

"It seems to me," said the psychologist, "that Mary is fairly well-adjusted at school. Perhaps we should look into the child's home situation."

"Mary is a happy, bright child," reported her mother. "maybe we should get together and ask Mary if she's having trouble with the other kids in school."

Finally Mother, the psychologist, the learning disabilities specialist, and the art teacher met with Mary.

"Tell us, Mary," the adults asked slyly, "if you wanted to draw a real straight line, what would you need?"

Expecting almost any answer, they were chagrined by her perky, "That's simple—a desk top that doesn't wiggle every time I write 'cause the bolts are loose!"

SPECIAL NOTE: This story always gets a laugh, perhaps because it strikes so accurately at the tendency to take a simple problem, with a simple solution, and make it complicated. It is best used when addressing a group gathered to be "problem solvers" as encouragement to take a straightforward, common-sense approach in their deliberations.

12

TOPICS:
Gaining perspective; taking the long view

AUDIENCE:
Suitable for all adult audiences

We had just finished dinner one evening and were in the process of clearing the table when my daughter addressed us.

"Mom and Dad," she said, "we all went down to the school nurse today, and she says that if you buy a special kind of soap, the lice in my hair should be gone in a couple of weeks."

We stopped clearing the table and froze, immobile.

"Oh, yes," continued our daughter, "and the dentist who examined our teeth told me that I'll need special braces, but they'll only cost four or five thousand dollars."

Somewhere, a dish fell to the floor.

"And after that," our child went on, "we cut class and went out in back of the gym and smoked some cigarettes that made me feel really funny. This big kid says he can get me more any time I want them."

We looked at each other, and our mouths dropped open and hung limply. It was a few seconds before we could speak.

"Honey," I finally managed to croak, "we . . . have to have a long talk . . ."

"I know," said my daughter, "but first I have to tell you something. I don't have lice in my hair. The dentist said that I have the straightest teeth he's ever seen. I would never cut class. And, I think you have to be a real dope to even try taking drugs. I never have and never will."

"Then, why . . ." we gasped in amazement.

"Well, Mom and Dad," she said producing a folded sheet of paper from her pocket, "I'm about to show you my report card, and I wanted to make certain that when you looked at it, you kept the whole thing in perspective.

SPECIAL NOTE: *This is a sure-fire story for getting plenty of laughs. Like most good humor, it is wrapped around a kernel of truth which touches our lives. Most of us have a great deal to be thankful for, and it is only right and just that we view our misfortunes in the perspective of our entire situation. This is most effective for dealing with large groups who are about to undertake a project.*

13

TOPICS:
Adult-child behavior; parents and children; influences
on children

AUDIENCE:
Adult audience composed of educators

Eddie was a bright enough child, and he usually answered the teacher's classroom questions correctly. The problem centered around the way in which he answered them.

Whenever the teacher asked him a question, Eddie would sigh deeply, scratch his head, and preface whatever answer he might give by a long, drawn out, "Weeeellll, now, let's see . . ."

On and on it went.

"Eddie, what is the capital of Maryland?"

"Weeeellll, now, let's see . . ."

"Eddie, how much is 26 times 11?"

"Weeeellll, now, let's see . . ."

"Eddie, what's the verb in this sentence?"

"Weeeellll, now, let's see . . ."

It was driving the teacher to distraction. Try as she might, she could not break Eddie of this habit. Even if she asked him what time it was, she could be certain that Eddie would tell her by beginning, "Weeeellll, now, let's see . . ."

Finally, she called in the boy's father and explained that Eddie, although a good student, had a certain habit she could not correct.

"Have you noticed anything peculiar about Eddie's speech?" she asked the boy's father.

"His speech?" replied the father as he began to scratch his scalp. "Weeeellll, now, let's see . . ."

SPECIAL NOTE: *Children are very quick to pick up the mannerisms and attitudes of adults, as this story points out. With teachers, this is a natural lead-in to a discussion of how our personal attitudes affect our students and the attitudes that we may be passing on to them.*

14

TOPICS:
Bad habits; point of view; husband-wife relations; perspective

AUDIENCE:
Adult audiences, particularly parents

A teacher I know was walking home one evening, when a tramp came up to him and asked if he could spare a dollar. The derelict was covered with dirt, his clothes in tatters, and it looked as if he hadn't bathed in months.

"If I give you a dollar," said the teacher, "you'll only go to the nearest bar and get a drink."

"No, sir," answered the tramp. "I don't drink."

"Well," responded the teacher. "then you'll just go gamble the money away."

"Oh, no, sir. I have never gambled in my life," said the tramp.

"Then, you'll buy cigarettes or a cigar or something equally unhealthy."

"I never touch tobacco," the tramp insisted.

"Let's see," said the teacher, "you don't smoke, you don't gamble, and you don't drink. Well, you're certainly unusual, I'll say that. I'll tell you what—I'll give you five dollars instead of one, and, what's more, I want to take you home for dinner."

Intrigued by the prospect of a free meal *and* five dollars, the tramp accompanied the teacher to his home. When they walked through the door, the teacher's wife was literally speechless. She soon recovered, however, and graciously prepared dinner for the three of them.

After dinner, the teacher gave the tramp a five dollar bill, and the fellow left.

Now it was his wife's turn. Turning to her husband, she began to berate him for what he had done.

"I know that it's a fine thing to be kind and charitable to those less fortunate than ourselves," she began, "but you didn't call ahead to tell me who you were bringing . What's more, I think that we're going to have to have the carpet and the chairs disinfected. I can understand your wanting to be kind, but why in the world did you have to choose someone as filthy as that to bring home?"

"Well, dear," her husband replied, "as he told you over dinner, the gentleman does not drink." And with that, he poured himself a glass of wine.

"He does not smoke." And the teacher lit up one of his favorite cigars.

"And, he does not gamble." And the husband turned to the football scores in the evening paper.

"I just wanted you to see," he added, "what kind of shape a man can get into when he has no bad habits!"

SPECIAL NOTE: *Instead of a teacher you could, of course, make the husband a member of any profession. This is another story that reminds us we must view everything in perspective. You might also try telling it as if you were the man who brought home the tramp. Either way, it never fails to get a good audience response.*

15

TOPICS:
A child's perception; misunderstanding; children

AUDIENCE:
Suitable for all adult audiences

One day, my six-year-old daughter came up to me to ask a question.

"Daddy," she said, "where was I born?"

"Honey," I answered, "you were born in Philadelphia, Pennsylvania."

"And where was Mommy born?" she continued.

"Mommy was born in San Francisco, California," I told her.

"And what about you, Daddy? Where were you born?"

"Sweetheart," I continued, "I was born in Houston, Texas. Would you like to see where those places are?"

With that, I got out an atlas and, turning to a map of the United States, I pointed out the locations of the three cities I had mentioned.

My daughter's eyes grew wide. "Wow, Daddy!" she exclaimed. "Look how far apart we were born. It's a real miracle how the three of us ever got together!"

SPECIAL NOTE: A child's simple perception of the world, and faith in the miracles it contains, can be the starting point for many discussions of the "miracles" of life we adults take for granted, such as the ability to question and to learn. It also points out how careful we, as educators, must be to preserve the sense of wonder that is inherent in every child.

16

TOPICS:
Patriotism; pride; challenges from the outside

AUDIENCE:
Suitable for all audiences

For his stay in the United States, the visiting Russian educator was housed with an American educator. On the Russian's first night here, the American teacher took him out to dinner at a local restaurant.

"You be calling this *bread*?" said the Russian pointing to the dinner rolls. "In Russia, we have bread so big it cover half this table!"

"What be this?" he said again when a large brook trout arrived for the entree. "Is so small! In Russia, we be calling this a minnow!"

"This be *coffee*?" he complained once more. "It be taking ten of these little cups to make one cup of Russian coffee!"

"Excuse me for a moment," said the American teacher who walked out to the lobby and called his son at home.

"Bobby," the American said, "don't ask any questions. Just go out to the back yard and get the pigeons from the coop and put them in the hall closet."

When the American and the Russian returned home, the American teacher said, "You can hang your coat in that closet, Ivan."

When Ivan opened the door, twenty startled pigeons flew out at him, fluttered frantically around the hallway, and finally flew out the open door, leaving Ivan wide-eyed against one wall.

"Really," said the American teacher in his most nonchalant voice, "I must do something about those *moths*!"

SPECIAL NOTE: *Nothing brings people together or engenders more pride than criticism from an outside source. You might use this story to point out the fact that we have much about which we can be legitimately proud, and it is well and good to appreciate that fact every once in awhile.*

Afterthoughts

All the stories in this chapter can be used effectively to break the ice and establish rapport in situations where you and your audience are strangers. There is, however, one secret to gaining rapport that has nothing to do with the stories you tell and that works better than any piece of humor. It is simply this: love your audience. If you expect to love your audience, if you expect them to love you, if you are enjoying yourself and can convey that fact to your audience, they cannot help but know it and return it in kind. In short, you get what you give. It has never failed us, and it will not fail you. Try it—it works.

Part 2
Stories That Make a Difference

If it is true, as the old Chinese proverb tells us, that "one picture is worth more than ten thousand words," then it is equally true that one well-chosen story that makes a point, and makes it with good humor so it will be remembered, must be worth more than ten thousand sermons. Indeed, it has been our experience that if we can make our point with good-natured humor or tell a story that particularly "touches" our listeners, then what we have to say will be remembered far longer and pondered more deeply than any amount of moralizing or preaching.

The stories you will find in this section have been specially chosen because they start people thinking even while they are smiling. The vast majority of them are humorous, and a few are poignant, but they are all crafted for getting your audience on your side and, possibly, acting as the basis for your speech to come. As such, they are invaluable to an educator.

When you hear the chuckle from your audience and see the appreciative nods of their heads, you will know that inwardly, in their minds and hearts, they are reacting to your story, and it has brought home the point you wanted to make.

17

TOPICS:
Making decisions; changing habits; creating our destiny; viewpoint

AUDIENCE:
Suitable for any adult audience

When I was teaching, I once shared a lunch hour with a young man who had just started his career in education. In those days, our school didn't have a cafeteria, so everyone "brown-bagged" it.

On Monday of the first week of school, the young man opened his lunch bag, examined the contents and exclaimed, "A tuna fish sandwich! I hate tuna fish sandwiches!" And he grumbled throughout the entire lunch period.

On Tuesday, the young man again extracted a sandwich from his bag and again exclaimed, "Tuna fish again! Oh, how I hate tuna fish!" And, again, he mumbled and complained of the evils of tuna fish all through lunch.

On Wednesday and Thursday, virtually the same scene was repeated. He would remove the wrapping from his sandwich, find tuna fish, and proclaim to the world his undying enmity for that particular food. Everyone in the faculty lounge was becoming very nervous, anticipating the next outburst.

On Friday, I decided that I had had enough, so when the young man removed a tuna fish sandwich and began what had become a daily tirade, I stopped him.

"Young man," I shouted, "if you dislike tuna fish so much, why don't you get a little backbone and simply tell your wife to make you some other kind of sandwich?"

The young man looked at me as if I had two heads.

"I don't know what you're talking about," he said. "I'm not married. I make my own lunches!"

SPECIAL NOTE: *Not only will this story occasion a good laugh from any audience, but it can be used as a springboard to all sorts of meaningful discussions. The point would seem to be that if we are unhappy with the results we are getting from our lives or from an educational method or program, or if any process we now use no longer works for us, then why do we insist on carrying on with the same old routine—why don't we change it? This is a particularly good story to use when you must introduce a new program or policy, using this as a springboard and going on to explain that you are instituting the new program not because it is new, but because it works better. In a very real sense, we all "make our own lunches" (happiness or unhappiness, et cetera), and this is an excellent story for pointing that out.*

18

TOPICS:
Point of view; optimism; looking at life; a child's
viewpoint

AUDIENCE:
Suitable for all audiences that can understand the
analogy

A mother and her two young daughters went to visit a neighbor.
While the two women visited inside, the girls were sent to play in
the neighbor's rose garden.

Very shortly, one of the girls came running in, her face wet with
tears.

"Oh, Mommie!" she wailed. "I've made a terrible discovery. All
of the roses have thorns!"

As Mother pacified the weeping child, the second daughter
skipped into the room, her face radiant and beaming.

"Oh, Mommie," she smiled, "come and see! I've made a
wonderful discovery. All of the thorns have beautiful roses!"

*SPECIAL NOTE: We'll share a secret with you—we can't write this story
without having tears come to our eyes. It bespeaks a very
basic philosophy about life that can often see us through
when times get rough. Whether our roses have thorns or
our thorns have roses depends largely on us. Wouldn't
it be a wonderful world if we could all see the roses. It's
within our grasp, if we work at it, and as educators, we
owe it to our students and ourselves to try very hard.*

19

TOPICS:
Creating destiny; what we can do; the value of
the individual

AUDIENCE:
Suitable for all audiences

On the day when our new refrigerator arrived, I was particularly busy, and I must tell you that I wasn't really paying that much attention. Therefore, when the delivery men asked me where they should leave the packing crate, I mumbled something about, "Just put it beside the house, and I'll get to it later."

Later, when I finally had time, I walked outside and was confronted by a huge cardboard-and-wood crate tilted against the side of our house.

What an eyesore! Not only that, but it would take me hours to break that thing apart for the garbage, and I probably would have to call someone to cart the thing away, at an extra cost, of course!

But, task led to task, and the afternoon passed until I chanced to look out our kitchen window and again spotted that monstrosity— but now it was in our backyard! Realizing that it hadn't walked there under its own power, I went out for a closer look.

As I approached, I noticed that the crate had undergone some changes. Holes were cut in the sides of it, and a large arch of cardboard was missing from one side. What's more, the happy sound of children's laughter echoed from it.

I looked through one of the cut openings. There was my son with several of his playmates, giggling happily, curled up in positions only children can achieve.

"Mom!" exclaimed my son. "Thank you, thank you! This is so great!"

"Thank me?" I said. "For what?"

"For this!" he said, stretching his arms.

"You're thanking me for a broken down, worn-out old crate?"

"No,", he sighed. "Thank you for THIS! When I got home from school, I saw it beside the house. It's the clubhouse we wanted, and sometimes it will be a fort or a castle or the secret place where the spies can't get you! Gosh, Mom, this is the best present I ever had!"

SPECIAL NOTE: *This is also one of our favorite stories, for it bespeaks the fact that we, ourselves, are responsible for what we make out of every situation. It serves as a very effective closing for a speech when you are embarking on a new project. Will that project (curriculum, class, conference, et cetera) succeed or fail, be a castle or an eyesore? Well, isn't it a matter of how we view it, and won't it be what we make of it?*

20

TOPICS:
Individual effort; rewards; the value of work

AUDIENCE:
Suitable for all audiences

A clergyman from the big city and his wife were on vacation, when he was invited to preach at a very small country church. As he entered the church, he dropped a dollar bill into the collection box.

He gave his sermon, and after the services were completed, the pastor of the church came up to him rather apologetically.

"Sir," said the pastor, "we are a small and a poor church, and it's impossible for us to pay you what we would like to for your fine sermon. However, we always give visiting clergymen whatever there is in the collection box."

With that, the collection box was opened, and a single dollar bill tumbled out.

"Just think," said the clergyman's wife, "if you had put in a twenty-dollar bill, you could have taken me to lunch on your earnings!"

SPECIAL NOTE: The point of this story is, of course, that we get back what we put in. In this way, it is similar to the point of the previous story. What we get out of teaching or a project or a conference depends to a large extent on how much WE, personally, put into it in terms of our efforts and commitment. We will get out of it in direct proportion to what we put into it.

21

TOPICS:
Job performance; the dignity of work; point of view

AUDIENCE:
Suitable for all audiences

A new church was under construction in our town, and as I passed by one day, I saw three workmen hard at their jobs preparing the stones for the walls.

I went up to the three workmen and asked, "What are you doing?"

The first workman looked up at me and snarled, "I'm working hard for my wages."

The second workman wiped sweat from his brow and said, "I'm chiseling granite."

The third workman beamed at me and smiled, "I'm helping to build a monument to God."

SPECIAL NOTE: Three workmen doing the same job, yet each sees it differently—who do you think is happiest? The answer is obvious, of course. The moral would seem to be that the perspective one takes in one's work is of great importance indeed. That's a very important lesson to remember when the pressures of the job get us down.

22

TOPICS:
Innovative solutions; investigating alternatives; quick thinking

AUDIENCE:
Suitable for all audiences

When I visited the county fair, one of the attractions that seemed to draw the most attention was the shooting gallery. The targets were balls that had been placed into a stream of air so that they moved and danced and rose and fell at uneven rates. As I watched, many people tried to hit those moving balls, but very few managed to get more than one out of every ten shots. I missed every shot I took.

As I was watching, a person came along and paid for his shots. He held the rifle, and for a good ten minutes, he did nothing but look at the targets. He stared and stared until people began to get uneasy.

Finally, in one swift motion, he drew the rifle into position, fired once, and every single ball fell to the ground. Everyone was amazed!

I couldn't help myself. I rushed up to him and began shaking his hand.

"Sir," I said, "that is the most amazing piece of marksmanship I have ever witnessed. How did you manage to do it?"

"Well," the man replied, somewhat embarrassed by all the attention he was getting, "I kept looking at them balls, and I noticed it was that thar motor on the side working the machine keeping them balls in the air. Well, heck, once I had that figured out, it didn't take nothing to see if I put a hole through that confounded motor, all them balls would just naturally fall."

SPECIAL NOTE: This gets a good laugh, particularly if you can deliver the last paragraph in an appropriate country accent. We have used this story to work into the fact that we must all be on our toes in looking for solutions to our problems and that, quite often, the solution is within the problem itself.

23

TOPICS:
Making a difference; children; working toward the future

AUDIENCE:
Suitable for all adult audiences, particularly educators

One day at the end of school, I was leaving the building when this brand new Cadillac pulled up. A young man jumped out and called my name.

He was wearing a three-piece suit that looked as if it had cost my weekly salary, patent-leather shoes, and a pure silk tie. Try as I might, I could not place him. When he told me who he was, my mouth dropped open.

"But . . . but . . ." I stammered, "when you went to this school, you always wore a torn T-shirt and dirty jeans. As I recall you rarely, if ever, did homework, and I must have kept you after school at least three-quarters of the year!"

"Yes, sir," said the sharply dressed young man. "That's why I came by this afternoon. I just wanted to thank you."

"Thank me?" I said. "For what?"

"Well," said the young man, "you didn't know it, but all through high school, I kept up this paper route, and every time you kept me after school, my mom made me put five dollars in a glass jar.

"I remember that every afternoon, you would sit back in your chair and say, 'You've got to get down to business; you have to get down to it!'"

"What has that got to do with anything?" I asked.

"Just this. When I graduated, I couldn't find a job, and then I remembered your telling me that I had to 'get down, get down!' So, I took the money from the jar, invested in a disco, and now I'm opening three more in other cities!

"I didn't realize it at the time, sir, but you were very good for me, and I just wanted to thank you for the advice!"

SPECIAL NOTE: *It is within the power of each and every one of us to make a difference in the lives of the children we touch. Even though we may not realize it at the time, the influence of one individual can make a difference, as this story points out. We have found that educators, in particular, relate to this message, and it's a very appropriate story for closing an address to teachers.*

24

TOPICS:
Teachers; teaching; views of teachers and teaching; value of teachers

AUDIENCE:
Suitable for all adult audiences, particularly educators

When one of our teachers retired recently after forty years in the classroom, there was a huge dinner for her. People flocked to the affair, not only colleagues and friends, but the numerous children, now grown to adulthood, whom she had taught over the years.

They all came and many of them spoke. They spoke of the teacher's kindness, of her understanding, her sternness in the classroom coupled with her love of her students, and the special care she took to see to it that every student learned. Many of her former students attributed their success in later life to the values and knowledge they had learned as students in her classes.

Finally, it was the teacher's turn to speak, and as the master of ceremonies introduced her, he remarked that perhaps she would be willing to share some of the secrets of her success in teaching.

"There's no secret to it," she said as she began to speak. "On my first day of teaching, forty years ago, I walked into the classroom to find that my students had placed a tack on my chair, put an apple with a worm in it on my desk, and someone had written on the board, 'You can't teach us nothing!'

"Since that day, I have always checked my chair before sitting down, never eaten anything given to me by a student, and made it my special project to see to it that every child in my class learned.

"You see, within five minutes of that first day, I knew that my bottom could stand the tack and my stomach could survive the worm—but I realized that my conscience would never forgive me if I taught them 'NOTHING!'"

SPECIAL NOTE: *This story could be used as a discussion topic, as a tribute to an educator, or as a device to start your audience thinking about the nature of education.*

25

TOPICS:

A child's view; adult interaction with children; love

AUDIENCE:

Suitable for all adult audiences

> My little girl came running up;
>   With twinkling eyes she said,
> "I love you best of all the world;
>   You're prettier than Fred!"
> And all the while upon her hand
>   Her pet, named Fred, just sat
> His whiskered jaw chewed noisily;
>   His scaley feet were flat;
> His gray-white fur stood up in scruffs;
>   His beady eyes were pink;
> And I can tell you this, my friends,
>   It really made me think!

SPECIAL NOTE: *Quite often, love is expressed in ways we don't relate to. A child is very quick to express feelings toward adults that adults may fail to understand. If we strive to love and care about children under our care, they will feel it and will respond in kind.*

26

TOPICS:
What we teach; helping; influences in children's lives

AUDIENCE:
Suitable for all adult audiences, particularly educators

It has been said that teachers are taught by their students. I'd like to share with you an incident that brought the truth of that statement home to me.

I was walking down the street of a local town recently, when I heard my name called. When I turned around, a young man whom I placed to be in his late teens or early twenties was coming up to me.

"I'm sure you don't remember me," he said, "but I remember you. Do you recall the day, about five or six years ago, when you covered the science class and talked about Gregor Mendel?"

I did remember. The science teacher had been taken ill suddenly, and since I was on hall duty at the time, I was asked to cover his class.

I teach English, and my knowledge of science is somewhat limited, so for a moment I was at a loss as to what to do with the class. Then I remembered the book I was reading at the time which was about Gregor Mendel, the monk who experimented with pea plants and discovered the laws of genetics. I thought it was fascinating, and I shared the story with that class. As I spoke to them about Mendel's experiments and his life, I became more and more wrapped up in the story, and I began drawing diagrams on the board and sharing my enthusiasm with them. When the bell rang, I dismissed the class and thought no more about it.

Now, six years later, the young man before me continued, "Well, I was in that class, and when you told us about Mendel's experiments, you just made it come alive. When the class was over, I was so excited, I went down to the library and got out the book you told us about. When that was finished, I got others. Anyhow, in June I'll be graduating from college with a degree in biology, and when I saw you, I wanted to say thanks for showing me the path."

And, with that, he melted back into the crowd. To this day, I do not know his name.

Later, I would read what Henry Adams wrote: "A teacher affects eternity; he can never tell where his influence stops."

I wish I could meet that young man again. Whoever he is and wherever he is, I would like to thank *him* for teaching *me* a lesson I will never forget.

SPECIAL NOTE: *This story goes over extremely well with any group of educators. It seems to express, in a very dramatic way, the fact that we do not teach subject matter, we teach children—and we can have a significant influence in each child's personal as well as academic life. This story serves as an inspiring challenge to educators to continue reaching out and influencing every child in our schools.*

27

TOPICS:
    Helping ourselves; seizing opportunities; individual effort

AUDIENCE:
    Suitable for all adult audiences

The rain had come down hard for many days, causing the river to flood its banks and inundate the countryside. Rescue crews were out, working full time to evacuate people whose houses lay in the path of the rising waters.

One boat spotted a house with the water up to the level of the front porch on which an old man was standing.

"Come on," shouted the rescue workers, "get in the boat!"

"Thank you," said the old man, "but I'll stay right here. The Lord will take care of me."

With that, the boat left. An hour later, they returned to find that the water had risen to the second story. This time, the old man stood in the window of his bedroom on the second floor.

"Please, sir," they shouted, "get in!"

"No," the old man insisted, "I'm staying put! I told you, the Lord will take care of me!"

The boat left again. An hour later, on their last sweep through the area, the boat again passed by the house. The water was now up to the rooftop, and there was the old man, perched on the roof, holding on to the chimney.

"Sir," they shouted from the boat, "the current is getting worse. We have to return to our base. Won't you please get into the boat?"

"Young man," the old man replied, "I told you before that the Lord will take care of me. Now, please leave."

With that, the boat and the rescue workers left. The old man sat on the roof, and eventually the waters rose, and he drowned.

When the old man got to heaven, the first thing he did was ask for an audience with God.

"Lord," said the old man, "I have a complaint to make. I always believed that you would take care of me. So how come you let me drown?"

"Man," said the Lord, "I don't know what you have to complain about. I did take care of you. After all, I sent you that boat three times!"

SPECIAL NOTE: *We do have to recognize our opportunities when they present themselves, don't we? Sometimes, opportunity stares us right in the face, and we refuse to "get on board." This is an excellent story for leading into a discussion of using the resources that are available to us rather than waiting around and complaining.*

28

TOPICS:

Quick thinking; innovation; taking different approaches

AUDIENCE:

Suitable for all adult audiences

A college professor gave an exam on which he asked the question, "Using only a barometer, how would you measure the height of the science building on this campus?"

Most students pondered the problem and wrote lengthy explanations involving taking readings of atmospheric pressure and figuring distance through mathematical computations.

One student, however, who may have been short on book knowledge but was definitely long on practicality and innovation, came up with an answer that even the professor could not dispute.

"I would take the barometer," he wrote, "and tie a string around it. I would stand on the roof of the science building, lower the barometer to the ground, then measure the string with a ruler."

In a conference with the lad sometime later, the professor pointed out that while the answer was certainly innovative, the boy intended to use a ruler and a string, while the question had required the use of only a barometer.

"If you can get around that," smiled the professor, "I'll give you full credit for your answer."

The young man thought for a moment and said, "That's easy, Professor. I take the barometer to the architect who designed and constructed the building. Then, I offer to give him one very fine, unused barometer if he'll look in his records and tell me how tall the science building was when finished. It's an offer he can't refuse!"

SPECIAL NOTE: When we are faced with a problem, sometimes we have to look beyond the boundaries of the problem in order to find the solution. This seems to be the message behind the laughter in this story, and it can be used to start discussions along this line.

29

TOPICS:
Children's needs; adult-child interaction; education of children

AUDIENCE:
Especially effective with audiences of parents and educators

It was Parents Day at our school. A program featuring songs and short skits had been prepared for the parents by the children, and they were in high spirits anticipating the day.

Attendance was marvelous! The auditorium was filled with parents who beamed with loving pride as their children performed. The parents of all my children were there. All, that is, except for one little boy who had no one in the audience.

As I thought about it, I realized that I had never met that boy's mother, even though it was late in the school year. She had not come to conferences or to the open house, and now she had missed the Parents Day presentation. In the back of my mind, an image of her was beginning to form, and it wasn't pleasant.

At the party that followed the performance, I sought out the child. Suddenly, I wanted to say something to him that might make up, however little, for his mother's nonattendance.

I don't think I did very well, because all I could think to say was, "Billy, I'm sure your mother had a very good reason why she couldn't be here today."

He looked up at me and said, "I know. She has to work. Ever since my dad got sick, Mom has been working so we can have money. She can't come to school during the day, but she helps me with my homework every night. On weekends, we always go to visit Dad in the hospital, and the three of us are together. Besides, she *is* here today. Look!"

Before I could say anything, he unbuttoned his shirt and spread it wide. I was greeted by the photograph of a smiling woman, attached to Billy's chest with adhesive bandages.

"Mom put that there this morning," Billy explained. "She said that even if she couldn't be here in person, I'd know that she was always there in my heart!"

What else could I do? I hugged the boy—I hugged him hard! But to this day, I don't think the youngster understood why my eyes filled with tears.

SPECIAL NOTE: *This story beautifully expresses the needs that all children share, and makes it evident that in meeting those needs, we are fulfilling our roles as parents and educators. This might also be used to point out that no one should be quick to judge others.*

30

TOPICS:
Kindness; reaping the rewards of what you do;
influencing the future

AUDIENCE:
Suitable for all audiences

Little Tommy was a holy terror in the classroom. It wasn't that the lad was bad or even mean-natured. He simply never stopped! From the first bell to the last, he was a whirlwind, getting up fourteen times to sharpen his pencil, waiting until the middle of the math lesson to exclaim that there was a bug on the floor, knocking over a stack of books during silent reading—the list went on and on!

What's more, his grades were suffering as his behavior ate away at his concentration on his schoolwork.

Then one afternoon after school, I was leaving the building when I heard loud shouts and noises coming from the playground. I went to investigate and found Tommy, surrounded by a group of bigger boys who were shoving him back and forth. I stopped the incident, took names, sent the boys on their way, and left for home.

The next day, Tommy was a different boy. He was actually helpful in class; he asked questions and answered those I asked him. Not once did he get up to sharpen a pencil, run in the room, or shout out and cause a commotion. We took a quiz, and he got B+!

I could not resist calling him to my desk just before dismissal.

"Tommy," I asked, "are you all right today?"

"Oh sure," he answered. "Today was fun. I really learned a lot. I gotta pay attention more often."

"I'm delighted to hear you say that," I told him, "but, let me be honest. You don't usually act as nicely as you did today. Why the change?"

"Well, you know those kids yesterday afternoon?"

"Yes."

"If you hadn't stopped them, they would have beat me up. I know I drive you crazy, but you were still nice to me and saved me.

So, I wanted to give you something for being so good. I thought and thought, and finally figured out a present that only I could give you."

Tommy smiled and leaned closer.

"I gave you a day of rest!"

SPECIAL NOTE: *This story, while on the surface evoking a smile, can be a good lead-in to a serious discussion of some truths about teaching. For example, you want your audience to consider that every action of a teacher, whether good, bad or "indifferent," has consequences far beyond the ability to perceive them. This, in turn, can lead your audience to a new awareness that, because teachers influence children in the formative years, they should treat their students as they would like to see their students treat others. Although we teachers may not see the results of our hard work firsthand, surely the world will be a better place because we gave it our best.*

Afterthoughts

All the entries in this section contained a message that was intended to reach your audience and start them thinking. Often, merely telling the story will be enough, for your audience will be taken by its message. Other times, you may wish to expand upon the message, making it relevant to your thoughts or to the task at hand. In either case, the story will be effective if, and only if, YOU truly believe in the message it conveys. YOUR sincerity is the key to making these stories effective and ensuring that they will have a lasting effect upon your audience. Told with sincerity and warmed by the fire of your own belief, these stories can and will make a difference in the lives of your listeners.

Part 3
Classroom Classics

So much happens in the day-to-day operation of the classroom, it is impossible to chronicle all of it. Yet anyone who has ever been there will tell you there are moments that stand out in every teacher's mind—those moments that are so poignant or funny or touching that they refuse to be forgotten with the passage of years.

These are the moments and memories on which this section is built. Here you will find stories and anecdotes that reflect the myriad interactions taking place in our nation's classrooms each and every day. Here are the sometimes meaningful, sometimes just-plain-funny events that make up the lighter side of today's educational scene.

There are literally hundreds of uses for these stories. Use them as part of any speech you are making to educators or parents, and they will be appreciated for their humor and warmth. Use them to drive home a point you are making. Or use them merely to break the ice and establish rapport. They are fit for all occasions.

We strongly recommend that you personalize these stories when you tell them. Use your own name in place of the teacher's or make it happen in your school or district. Such personalization adds familiarity to the situation and, quite often, makes it better received by your audience.

May we also hope that these stories will bring a smile to your face as they take you back to your days in the classroom and those special moments that happened to you and that are your own personal classroom classics.

31

TOPICS:
Economics; taxation; faith; a child's perception of the
adult world

AUDIENCE:
Suitable for all adult audiences

As part of a study of the federal government, the teacher had
arranged for the class to be addressed by a member of the Internal
Revenue Service. The gentleman spoke at length about taxes and
taxation, how taxes are assessed, how they are collected, where the
money goes, and so on.

"I firmly believe," the man concluded, "that American citizens
do not mind paying taxes; I believe that every wage earner cheerfully
pays his taxes to his government; I believe that taxpayers make out
their returns fairly and are anxious to pay what they fairly owe. Now,
do you have any questions?"

One little boy in the back of the room raised his hand.

"Mister," the lad asked, "do you also believe in the tooth fairy?"

SPECIAL NOTE: *The unexpected ending of this story always brings a large
laugh from any audience. We heard this story used effectively in a speech on the school budget. It might well
belong in any address concerned with economic matters.*

32

TOPICS:
SEX—need any more be said?

AUDIENCE:
Adults—goes over well with parents and/or educators

NOTE:
The adult world of sex and children's misconceptions about it have formed the basis for literally hundreds of jokes and anecdotes. The stories that follow are our personal favorites. They have been chosen not only because they are inoffensive and suitable for any audience but also because they reflect children's viewpoints on this adult subject.

In the sex education class, the teacher was discussing the pressures that teenagers often undergo in this very important area.

"I know what you mean," said a senior girl. "You can't believe the pressure and stress I'm under right now."

"Would you want to explain?" asked the teacher.

"Well," said the girl, "it's just that all I hear lately is 'Get married; move away from home and have kids.' Over and over and over again, 'Get married; move away from home and have kids!' It's driving me crazy!"

"I agree," said the teacher. "That's a terrible position for your boyfriend to put you in."

"Boyfriend?" exclaimed the young lady. "It's not my boyfriend who's saying that—it's my parents!"

*   *   *

Two grade-school children were talking in the school playground.

"I had a talk with my father last night," said one of them, "about where babies come from. He told me that a daddy plants a seed inside a mommy, and then the baby grows in the mommy's tummy until it gets ready to come out."

"That's dumb," said the other child. "Everybody knows that the stork brings the baby and leaves it all wrapped up in the mailbox!"

"Of course I know that," said the first youngster, "but you know how it is with parents—sometimes you just have to humor them!"

*   *   *

The class was looking at slides of baby animals, and after the presentation, the teacher asked the class if there were any questions. One little boy raised his hand.

"All those baby animals," said the lad, "had to begin somewhere. So, what I want to know is where did I begin?"

The teacher drew a deep breath. She realized that this was an honest question, and she wanted to give the boy an honest answer that would be within his ability to understand.

"Well, Billy," she began, "we all started the same way. We start either as an egg or as a seed."

"Yes," said Billy, "but, which one?"

"It doesn't matter," said the teacher.

"Sure it does," asserted Billy. "Otherwise, how do you know if you're a bird or a daffodil?"

*   *   *

"Daddy," said the little girl, "where did I come from?"

Daddy sighed deeply, and it passed through his mind that his little girl was growing up. He also affirmed what he considered to be his deep responsibility to provide his daughter with accurate and sensible knowledge in this area. Therefore, he sat down with his child and began to explain truthfully and simply the "facts of life" she had wanted to know.

"Now, honey," he said when he was finished, "do you understand?"

"Yeah, Daddy," she said. "Thank you."

"Any time, sweetheart," her dad remarked, "but could you tell me what made you ask?"

"Sure, Dad. Billy Fredricks asked me where I came from, and I didn't know. Boy, wait 'til I tell him this! He actually thinks he came from Philadelphia!"

SPECIAL NOTE: *The straightforward simplicity of children as contrasted with the complexity we adults sometimes weave into our lives and thinking continues to be a never-ending source of enjoyment and laughter. It should be noted, however, that the issue of sex education in the schools is usually one that is highly charged with emotion. It would not be a good idea, therefore, to "joke" about the matter if faced with an audience whose thinking on the subject is diametrically opposed to yours.*

33

TOPICS:
Perceptions; questions and answers; teacher-student interaction

AUDIENCE:
Excellent for adult audiences of parents and educators

A group of parents and school administrators was touring an elementary school in the district, and stopped in at a second grade classroom where the teacher was conducting a drill in arithmetic.

"Mickey," she asked, calling on one tousle-haired youngster, "how much is eight minus three?"

The boy bit his lower lip, cast his eyes toward the ceiling, and said, "Five!"

"Mickey," beamed the teacher, "that was a very good answer."

"Very good, my eye!" rejoined Mickey. "Hell, ma'am, that was perfect!"

SPECIAL NOTE: *You could use this story effectively to point out the fact that something which, to an adult, may seem simple and uncomplicated may be very difficult to a child, requiring that child's complete concentration and effort. Perhaps it might be well to remember this and give praise where it is due.*

34

TOPICS:
Misconceptions; the humorous answers of students
on tests

AUDIENCE:
Older students and adults, particularly parents

NOTE:
The following definitions are taken from test answers
given by children in various grades.

The difference between a pencil and a pen is that when you try
to sharpen a pen you get detention for two nights.

* * *

General Sherman said, "War is heck." (Dear Miss Foley, I know
he said the other word, but I'm too young to say it. You have to be
a general with a beard before people think it's okay when you curse.)

* * *

Apples are nutritious and, except when my sister bakes them in
a pie, very tasty.

* * *

I would say that one of the reasons for the decline of the Roman
Empire was Latin. They probably died of boredom trying to
memorize verb declensions.

* * *

A microorganism is like when you plug your electric organ into
a microphone.

* * *

If they would have had cameras in Russia during the middle
ages, Peter the Great would have been a movie Tsar.

* * *

The great Art Masters were Art Carney and Art Linkletter, and that's all I can think of right now.

* * *

A well-balanced meal is one that won't slip off your lap at one of those buffet things.

* * *

The early settlers suffered a lot when they crossed through the open deserts and the rough mountains. I don't see why they didn't just stay on Interstate 80.

* * *

A politician is a man who talks on television and makes my daddy's face turn red.

* * *

The homework question is, "What do you call a man who marries and supports more than one woman?" Well, I asked my dad, and he said, "Crazier than a bedbug!" Is that the right answer?

* * *

A Rough Rider is somebody who doesn't get the shock absorbers checked regularly.

* * *

A census taker is a man who goes from house to house increasing the population.

SPECIAL NOTE: Many individuals have, over the years, been kind enough to supply us with these definitions from student test papers. They can be used effectively in speeches or merely to share a laugh or two. Parents seem to enjoy them most of all.

35

TOPICS:
Fairy tales; a child's view; the real world and
imagination

AUDIENCE:
Suitable for all adult audiences, particularly parents

It was story time, and the first grade teacher was telling her class
the story of the princess and the frog.

". . . so," she continued, "the beautiful princess took the frog
up to her room, and that night, before she went to bed, she kissed
the little frog goodnight. The next morning, when the princess
awoke, the little frog had changed into a handsome prince. And, the
prince and princess were married, and they lived happily ever after."

All the children clapped their hands in glee, except for one little
girl who sat with a deeply knitted brow.

"Karen," said the teacher, "what's wrong? Didn't you like the
story?"

"Oh, I liked it, all right," answered Karen. "I was just wondering—if you were her mother, would you believe a story like that?"

*SPECIAL NOTE: Between childhood and adulthood lies a gulf of wonder
and belief that becomes somewhat shrouded as we grow
older. This story seems to recognize that fact and can be
used to lead into a discussion of children's perceptions
of life and the world around us.*

36

TOPICS:
Parental worries; the problems with young people

AUDIENCE:
Suitable for adult audiences, particularly parents and educators

Let's face it—we all get fed up with our kids sometimes. Oh, we love them, but there are times when they try our patience.

I must have felt that way one day when I was complaining to my father about the troubles of raising children. He went to another room for a moment and returned with a scrap of paper.

"I think it's time you read this," he said.

I carefully unfolded the old paper and found that it was a letter. I read: "I have no idea of the proper course of action. I have labored to instill in my son a sense of moral values, but I fear that it has been to no avail. The boy is lazy and does not wish to work a sensible twelve-hour day. He wishes to find employment where he will have Saturday as well as Sunday to himself! I found the sheet music to a ragtime song (the devil's music) in the piano bench. He even believes that some day men will fly like birds and buggies will roll without horses! Can you imagine such idiocy! Now, the worst of the lot, he wishes to make his own decision as to a wife rather than take the sage advice of his loving parents. I would appreciate any advice you could give me, as I am at a loss to determine what next to do."

"That letter, from one friend to another," said my father when I had finished reading, "was written by your great-grandfather about your grandfather. I want you to have it now, but only if you'll promise to give it to your son when he starts complaining one day."

SPECIAL NOTE: This story never fails to draw a smile. Use it to show that the generations were in conflict many years ago as well as today. It points out that perceptions of what constitutes a problem change with time.

37

TOPICS:
Honesty; a child's perception of the world; education

AUDIENCE:
Suitable for all adult audiences

Soon it would be Jimmy's first day of school. His mother and father had taken pains to prepare their son and to make certain he developed a very positive attitude that would serve him well in his education. They had played "school" with the child, rehearsing him and emphasizing the fun he would have.

The first day of school came, and with a lump in their throats, the mom and dad sent their son off to begin his academic career, hoping that they had given him a firm foundation for success.

Their fears were greatly allayed when Jimmy returned home from his first day filled with the wonder of the place. He spoke incessantly of the "nice" teacher, all the boys and girls he had met, and all the "great" activities they had done. He even presented Mommie with a picture he had drawn specially for her.

Needless to say, his mom and dad were overjoyed.

The following day, Jimmy's mother went to his bedroom and woke him gently.

"Come on, Jimmy," she said when the child had awakened, "get dressed. It's time for school."

Suddenly, Jimmy's face twisted into a paroxysm of pain, and tears began to stream down his face.

"Jimmy!" exclaimed his mother, "What's the matter?"

"Oh, no!" bawled Jimmy. "You mean I have to do it again?"

SPECIAL NOTE: Use this story to very humorously bring out the fact that while adults may know the full details of what is happening, a child may see only one step at a time. This story will literally "bring down the house" when told to an audience of parents of elementary schoolchildren.

38

TOPICS:
Telling the truth; a child's view of honesty; quick thinking

AUDIENCE:
Suitable for all adult audiences

The teacher had been strenuously emphasizing the need for honesty and always telling the truth, when one day she had the opportunity for a practical exercise in the topic.

Returning from recess, the teacher found three of her charges who had come in from the playground earlier than the others. All three looked extremely guilty, and the teacher noticed pennies lying on the floor next to the wall. While a minor form of gambling, indeed, the practice of "pitching pennies" was discouraged by the school. She suspected these three boys had been doing just that.

"I'm going to ask you a question," she said, "and I want you to remember what we have been saying in class about telling the truth. Now, Tommy Smith, were you pitching pennies?"

"N-N-No," he lied, "I wasn't pitching pennies!"

"Billy Jones," said the teacher, turning to the second boy, "were you pitching pennies?"

"Ma'am," he gulped, the words sticking in his throat, "I wasn't pitching no pennies!"

With that, the teacher turned to the third boy.

"Jimmy Brown," said the teacher, "I know you're an honest boy, and I want you to tell me the truth. Were you pitching pennies?"

Jimmy agonized within himself, and finally a smile lit his face.

With his hands outstretched, palms upward, and with a knowing glance at the other two boys, he looked directly at the teacher, and said, "Pitching pennies, ma'am? With *whom?*"

SPECIAL NOTE: *The only way to cure lying is to take the advantage out of it. This story can be used to point this out and to emphasize how children view the subject.*

39

TOPICS:
Athletics; students and coaches; the school sports program

AUDIENCE:
Suitable for older students, parents, and educators

"All right, Jones!" shouted the coach, "I want you to go out on that field and BLOCK THAT KICK at all costs! Do you understand? Get that ball, and be smart about it. Use your head, Son, use your head!"

Would you believe, it took doctors an hour to remove that football from the boy's mouth!

* * *

Two high school girls met one night while they were out with their respective dates.

One girl whose date was the star player on the high school basketball team began to extol the virtues of her boyfriend to the other young lady.

"Ralph is very special," she said. "He can pass, block, steal the ball, and make fantastic 'slam-dunks.' It's just that he has a little trouble with his G-R-A-D-E-S!"

SPECIAL NOTE: We thought awhile before including these stories. While they always get laughs at athletic dinners and sports awards activities, they could do a disservice to our coaches and athletes who are, for the most part, highly intelligent people, managing both academic and sports careers with equal grace. It would be a good idea to point this out in any follow-up speaking you may do on the topic.

40

TOPICS:

Quick thinking; misunderstanding; teacher-student interaction

AUDIENCE:

Suitable for all adult audiences

After the class had spent some time learning about the animal kingdom, the teacher gave a quiz. One by one, she called on each child in the class, held up a picture, and asked the student to identify the creature depicted.

"Mary," the teacher asked while holding up a photograph, "what is this?"

Mary looked closely and guessed, "An armadillo?"

"Sorry, Mary," said the teacher, "but I can't give you credit for that answer. This is a picture of a tufted titmouse."

"Teacher," responded Mary, "can't you give me half credit? After all, I knew it wasn't a bird!"

SPECIAL NOTE: Words that have shades of meaning for adults often do not carry the same subtle distinctions for children. Consequently, we must take particular care to be precise and staightforward in speaking to our students. This story might well be used to bring out this point.

41

TOPICS:
Shades of meaning; misunderstanding; vocabulary

AUDIENCE:
Suitable for all adult audiences, particularly parents

The teacher was trying to build the vocabulary of her class. Therefore, she purposely used words the children were not familiar with, and then she would define them.

For instance, when it was story time, she told the class, "Children, I am going to tell you a narrative."

When the students looked at her questioningly, she explained, "That means a tale."

Then, as the class was leaving for recess, she told one boy, "Stanley, please extinguish the lights. Extinguish means to put out."

Later that day, when it came time for show and tell, one student anxiously raised his hand. He walked to the front of the room, eager to show off his new vocabulary.

"Last night before we went to bed," he said, "I grabbed the cat by the narrative and extinguished him!"

*　　*　　*

The vocabulary word was posterior. I explained to the class that a possible synonym was the word back. The posterior of something was its back.

"Now," I asked, "can anyone use the word in a sentence?"

One little boy raised his hand, and I called on him.

"I can use it in a sentence," he said. "When you turn around to write on the blackboard, we all get a good view of your posterior!"

SPECIAL NOTE: *Rote learning without understanding is no learning at all, as these two stories point out. You can also use these stories as examples of how children often do not perceive shades of meaning.*

42

TOPICS:
Fighting; children's arguments; peer interaction

AUDIENCE:
Suitable for audiences of parents and educators

When the class bully stepped up to the new student, a ring of children formed around them.

"I don't like your face," threatened the bully. "I'm gonna change it with my fists. What do you think about that?"

"Actually," said the new boy, "I think that we may possibly have a failure to communicate. I know that all disagreements can be settled in a civilized and gentlemanly manner, and I would be happy to enter into a dialogue with you on these points."

"What did he say?" the bully asked, looking around at the circle of children.

At this point, the new student unleashed a right cross which caught the off-guard bully squarely on the chin and sent him to the ground in a heap.

"Of course," said the new boy, standing over the bully, "first I will need your undivided attention!"

*   *   *

"Miss Jones, come quick!" shouted the small boy to his teacher. "There are two kids fighting on the playground, and somebody told me to come in here and get you to break it up!"

"Who sent you in to get me?" asked the teacher.

"The kid on the bottom!" said the student.

*   *   *

Young Harry was always getting into trouble for fighting, so much so that his mother had had several conferences with the principal and the guidance counselor.

"Harry," his mother told him, "I don't want you fighting. If you fight again, young man, you are going to be in serious trouble."

Harry did try. A week went by without a fighting incident, and then two and three passed without incident. It looked as if young Harry had finally learned to keep out of trouble.

One afternoon as school was letting out for the day, one of Harry's classmates came running up to him on the playground.

"Your mother!" shouted the classmate in the age-old taunt of schoolboys scrapping for a fight.

Harry was on him in an instant, and a few seconds later, Harry had the boy on the ground and was sitting on his chest.

"Now," shouted Harry, "what did you say about my mother?"

"Y-y-your mother," sobbed the boy on the bottom, "your mother . . . your mother sent me to get you. She's standing over there with a present for you, because you stopped fighting!"

SPECIAL NOTE: Children fight—that's a fact of life for all educators. This story would best be used to make that point. But follow it up with mention of the wonderful capacity children have, or so it seems, to forget their differences once the altercation is over. We often think it would be better if adults could adopt the same attitude. And that is a very good message for your audience to take away with them.

43

TOPICS:

Poor communications; adult misunderstanding of children

AUDIENCE:

Adult audience, especially parents

The teacher noticed that little Mary had seemed particularly upset all day long. When the final bell rang, she took Mary aside and asked what the trouble was.

"Mommie is taking me to the dentist this afternoon," said Mary, "and I'm scared!"

With this, the teacher began to comfort Mary and gently explained that there was nothing to fear from the dentist, that the dentist helped children keep their teeth healthy, and that Mary would be happy to have good teeth. Finally, the teacher concluded, "If you are big and brave and don't cry or make a fuss at the dentist's office, tomorrow I'll give you a new pencil box."

The following day, Mary presented herself at the teacher's desk and asked for her pencil box.

"I didn't cry or shout or nothing," proclaimed Mary.

"That's a big girl!" said the teacher. "What did the dentist do to you?"

"He didn't do nothing to me," said Mary. "I only had to go because my mommie couldn't find a sitter. But, he pulled two of my brother's teeth, and I didn't cry once!"

SPECIAL NOTE: *One point that can be made with this story is the fact that we had better make certain we understand exactly what a child MEANS, not just what he or she may be SAYING. There is many a misunderstanding between what a child says and what a child means.*

Afterthoughts

While the stories in this chapter represent the lighter side of the classroom, we are willing to wager there is an expert who has an even wider stock of stories drawn from real life that will delight any audience—and that expert is *you*. Any educator who thinks back upon his or her years with children can come up with scores of stories about incidents that enlivened the day and that still bring forth a smile when remembered. These can be the basis for even more personalized "classroom classics" with which to entertain and touch your audience.

Part 4
Blunders, Bloopers, and Puns

One philosophy we have heard describes life as "a tragedy to those who feel and a comedy to those who think." Nowhere does this seem more appropriate than in the area of those unthinking blunders and mistakes that we all make from time to time. While they may cause us embarrassment and frustration when they occur, with the passage of time we can often look back and smile, if not fondly then at least appreciatively, at these small blunders. Indeed, some of the most delightful humor we have ever known has centered around the goofs committed unwittingly by all sorts of people in all sorts of situations.

This is the material that forms the basis of this section. Here you will find those "slips of the tongue" and errors of judgment that often add zest and laughter to the educational scene. Many of them are drawn from true life situations, and all of them will find appreciative audiences among parents and educators who, we are certain, have their own supply of blunders and bloopers from which to draw.

We are also including in this section a good supply of puns. A pun may be, as someone once said, the lowest form of humor, but it seems also to be the one most memorized and "passed on" as well. We have told most of the outrageous puns in this section to faculty and parent groups. They were met with loud groans followed by laughter followed by applause followed, inevitably, by a request to "tell it again" so the listeners would be certain to get it right when they told it.

We are certain that you will find laughter here. Enjoy!

44

TOPICS:
Mathematics; observation; theory; proving a point

AUDIENCE:
Suitable for all adult audiences and older students

As an assignment, the members of the math class had to take a mathematical theorem and be able to prove it to the class.

When it came Jimmy's turn, he walked slowly to the front of the room and began to tell a very strange story.

Jimmy's father and uncle, it seemed, were very close, and they often liked to visit with each other's family. This did not happen too often, because Jimmy's uncle lived 500 miles away, but the two brothers got together every chance they could.

Then Jimmy's uncle joined the local Lions Club, and by telephone urged Jimmy's father to do the same where he lived. Jimmy's dad did join the group and enjoyed it very much.

Both men worked hard and soon, each man was elected secretary of his club. The next year, each became vice-president, and the year after that, president, of his Lions Club.

This kept both men very busy, and whenever one was free to visit, the other was not because of some club business.

Years went by without the brothers ever being able to visit, yet because each was president of the local Lions Club, club business came first, and they could not get together.

At this point the teacher interrupted.

"Jimmy," she said, "what has all this got to do with math and the proving of theorems?"

"Teacher," said Jimmy, looking amazed, "this *is* a proof. Surely you know the theorem that parallel Lions never meet!"

SPECIAL NOTE: *That "Parallel LINES never meet" has been discussed since the days of Euclid, but this is certainly a novel approach to its proof. Use this for fun or as part of a speech reminiscing about days in the classroom.*

45

TOPICS:
Science; the law; morality; approaches to a subject

AUDIENCE:
Suitable for all adult audiences and older students

"It is theoretically possible," explained the science teacher, "to take a single cell from a human being and by a process called *cloning*, to make an exact replica of the original human. This replica would be called a *clone*."

The teacher also pointed out that there were many opinions about cloning, and that some people regarded it as morally wrong. He then asked the class to think of various moral issues that might be raised concerning clones and cloning and be prepared to discuss them the next day.

On the following day, the teacher asked if anyone had come up with a moral issue concerning the subject, and one girl raised her hand.

"What if a man," she said, "wanted a son but was never married and couldn't adopt. So, he went to a scientist and had himself cloned.Pretty soon, he was presented with a baby boy who was, in reality, his clone.

"Now let's say that the boy grows up, and when he is about seven or eight years old, he begins to use obscene language. The father has always been a very proper man, and the use of obscenities by his son really upsets him. It gets so bad, in fact, with the little clone using more and more obscene language, that the father decides he cannot have the boy around any more.

"One day, when the man and his clone are in the mountains, the boy starts using obscene language, and in a fit of rage, the man pushes the boy over the edge and the clone falls 500 feet to his death.

"When the man gets back to his house, the police are there, and they arrest him. Would they arrest him for murder since he killed a human being, or would they arrest him for suicide since the clone was a replica of himself?"

"That's easy," called out a boy from the back of the room, "they wouldn't arrest him for either one."

"Oh," said the teacher, "then what would they arrest him for?"

"Simple," said the boy. "They'd arrest him for making an obscene clone fall!"

SPECIAL NOTE: *This is a groaner, all right. It does, however, draw a very big laugh. You might also use it as an introductory ice-breaker for a speech on the moral issues of education or any particular subject where issues of this type are raised.*

46

TOPICS:
Bragging; Christmas; holiday song; creating a scene

AUDIENCE:
Suitable for all adult audiences and older students

One of the teachers in our school was a real chess enthusiast. Whenever he had a free moment, you would see him with his pocket chess board working out some problem. He had participated in several local chess tournaments and had done very well indeed.

One December he was entered in a large chess tournament which was held in a rather fancy downtown hotel. It was the weekend just before Christmas, and I went to see him play.

He did very well, but his last match of the evening ended in a draw. I stayed around afterward to congratulate him, but when he came out into the foyer of the hotel, which was one of those large, open places that give a feeling of the outdoors, he was still with his opponent of the evening. They were arguing vigorously.

"If I didn't have a touch of the flu," said the opponent, "I would surely have beaten you!"

"Never!" exclaimed the teacher. "I'm better than you. I'm better than Bobby Fischer or any of the Russians!"

"No, you're not!" screamed the opponent. "I am!"

"No, I am!" shouted the teacher.

At which point the hotel manager came over and began to usher them out of the foyer.

"I don't care if it *is* almost Christmas," said the manager. "If there's one thing I can't stand, it's chess nuts boasting in an open foyer!"

SPECIAL NOTE: This is an excellent pun to use at a holiday get-together or dinner. It is also well-used with students who are familiar with the song and its opening line of "Chestnuts roasting on an open fire. . ."

47

TOPICS:
Critical thinking; children; revenge; science

AUDIENCE:
Suitable for all audiences, especially parents

The teacher was explaining to the elementary class about rabies and how harmful it could be. She explained that people who were bitten by a rabid dog could die if they were not treated in time. She also explained that, left untreated, the disease often caused people to go mad, and that the bite of an infected person could be just as bad as that of the rabid dog. All this she did to drive home the fact that if they were ever bitten, they should immediately go for medical help.

"Now," asked the teacher, "what would you do if you were bitten by a rabid dog?"

One little girl raised her hand and the teacher called on her.

"I'd go to my room and get out a pencil and paper," the child said.

Thinking she understood the child's reasoning, the teacher said, "Mary, it's very nice that you would want to write a will, but weren't you listening? Nowadays they have medicine that can cure rabies."

"I was listening, teacher," answered Mary, "but I wasn't going to write a will. I just thought that before I went for my shots, I'd make out a list of the people I wanted to bite first!"

SPECIAL NOTE: An audience of parents is especially receptive to this story. Perhaps because it so humorously reflects the fact that children often see things quite differently than adults—and that they have their own priorities!

48

TOPICS:
Value of money; children; finance; parents

AUDIENCE:
Particularly good with parents

One man I know was anxious to teach his daughter the value of money so, for her birthday, he gave her twenty-five dollars on the condition that she start her own bank account with it.

The daughter agreed, and the next day the proud father took his nine-year-old to the local bank where the vice-president of the bank, a father himself, made quite a fuss over this new account. He ushered the girl and her father into his office, and began to help her fill out the application.

Everything went fine until they came to one question on the application form.

"What was the name of your previous bank?" asked the vice-president.

The little girl frowned for a moment, then smiled deeply at her father.

"Piggy!" she announced proudly.

SPECIAL NOTE: Something that has one meaning to adults may take on a completely different perspective when seen through the eyes of a child. Use this story to illustrate that point as well as to get a warm laugh.

49

TOPICS:
Checking the facts; errors; miscommunication

AUDIENCE:
Suitable for all adult audiences

The new guidance counselor believed in good public relations, so when he spotted one outstanding report card among the pile on his desk, he immediately typed a letter.

"Jane is an outstanding student," he wrote. "Her grades are marvelous, and every teacher loves having her in class. She is a credit to herself and to her home. Jane has a bright future ahead of her. You must be extremely proud of Jane."

And he sent the letter off.

A few days later, the counselor received a reply in the mail and opened it.

"I *am* extremely proud of Jane," he read, "and I am pleased to know that she is doing so well in class. She really seems to be a marvelous student. However, my daughter's name is Mary, and I was wondering if you could tell me how *she* is getting on in school?"

SPECIAL NOTE: *We use this to point out that however well-intentioned we may be, we must take practical matters, such as checking our facts, into consideration as well. Both educators and parents seem to like this story.*

50

TOPICS:
Social studies; directions; innovative thinking

AUDIENCE:
Suitable for all adult audiences and older students

The social studies teacher had just finished a unit on directions.

"For your assignment," he said, "I want you to pick any three states in the atlas and write out the locations of their capitals by using directions."

One ingenious student was all ready the next morning.

"The capital of New Jersey," he read from his paper, "is southwest of the J; the capital of New York is northwest of the N; and Harrisburg, the capital of Pennsylvania, is directly between the feet of the last A!"

SPECIAL NOTE: *Whether educators or not, most people in your audience have likely experienced an assignment of this type where they failed to make their directions clear enough to be understood by all. Unfortunately, this is often discovered only after completion of the assignment! This story will be appreciated by educators and noneducators alike.*

51

TOPICS:

Sex; fathers and sons; the facts of life; plans going astray

AUDIENCE:

Suitable for all adult audiences, particularly parents

There came that inevitable time when Mother strongly suggested to Father that he tell their growing son the so-called facts of life. Father took this very seriously and set about thinking of the best way in which to impart this information to his son.

It was the spring of the year, when nature begins the age-old process of renewal, and the father hit upon what he considered to be just the right plan. He had to pick up some paint from the hardware store, and he would take his son along. On their way back, he would suggest they stop off at the local park. Once there, he would be able to show his son the flowers blooming, baby birds being hatched, the bees buzzing—everything that would gently help him tell about the miracle of reproduction in just the right setting.

The man's eyes welled with tears at the sublime beauty of it all, and soon he and his son were off on their errand.

Still somewhat starry-eyed, he drove with his son to the hardware store. As he paid for the paint, the man could hardly wait until they would be on their way again.

Just then, his son ran up to him with something in his hand.

"Hey, Dad," the boy yelled, "do you want to know why they call this a female plug?"

SPECIAL NOTE: *The best laid plans . . . et cetera, et cetera. This story also points out that children quite often learn things in ways that we, as adults, can hardly imagine—and certainly never intended.*

52

TOPICS:
Lying; parent-teacher relations; avoiding the
inevitable

AUDIENCE:
Suitable for adult audiences, particularly educators

The teacher called up the parents of one of her charges.

"Hello, Mrs. Smith," she said, "this is Billy's teacher. Might I
drop by on Monday night to talk to you and Mr. Smith about Billy?"

"I'm so sorry," answered Mrs. Smith, "but we have a previous
engagement on Monday."

"Oh? Well, then, how about Tuesday evening?"

"Uh . . . that's a bad day. Mr. Smith and I are going out of town
on Tuesday.

"All right, then would Wednesday evening be more convenient
for you?"

"I can see you're just not going to give up. All right, damn it,
make it Monday at seven-thirty!"

SPECIAL NOTE: *There is a moral here that is especially appropriate for an
audience of educators. Nobody wants to receive bad
news. If parents have come to associate the teacher's
phone call only with news of what's wrong with their
children, they maybe it's time we started calling and telling them what's RIGHT about their children as well.*

53

TOPICS:
History; a child's perspective; art; approach to a
subject

AUDIENCE:
Suitable for all adult audiences

The art teacher had just finished telling her class about the lives
of several famous artists. Now, she gave them an assignment for
homework.

"I want each of you to pretend to be one of the artists we talked
about," she said. "You are to write a letter to someone as if you were
the artist writing. Make certain that you tell something about your
life in the letter. And be sure that it is a friendly letter."

The children set about their task, and the next day the entire
class was ready with their letters. All was going fine until one young
man stood up and read his letter.

"Dear Mom and Dad," he read, "Do you remember those real
expensive earmuffs you promised to get me for my birthday? Boy,
have I ever saved you money! Signed, your son, Vincent van Gogh!"

SPECIAL NOTE: Teachers generally get a kick out of this story, for it is
so reflective of many children's perspectives of historical
events.

54

TOPICS:
Notes from home; home-school communication

AUDIENCE:
Suitable for all audiences, particularly educators

NOTE:
Over the years, so many people have shown us or told us about notes they have received from home, that it has been impossible to keep count. Recounted below are some examples, all reported to be actual letters, received by teachers from parents.

Dear Miss Jones,
Johnny was late because he was practicing on the drums my mother-in-law sent him. I swear I'll get even with that old bag some day!

* * *

Dear Miss Jones,
Please excuse Billy for being. It was definitely his father's fault!

* * *

Dear Miss Jones,
Mary told me that you kept her after school because she did not know her Gettysburg address. This was totally unfair, since we have no address in Gettysburg and have never lived there!

* * *

Dear Miss Jones,
Please don't tell Harry that he needs a bath. Harry smells like his father. You just don't know what a man smells like!

* * *

Dear Miss Jones,
Jack has often spoken very highly about you and told us what a fine teacher you are. He also showed us the snapshot he took of

you. He says you are a dedicated teacher. I read somewhere that many educators believe you can't be an effective teacher until you are married and have children of your own. I am certain, from all that Jack has told us, that you want to be the finest teacher possible. So, I'd like to tell you a little about Jack's older brother, the lawyer . . .

*   *   *

Dear Miss Jones,

I got your note on Jimmy's behavior in class. Jimmy is just like his father. I rest my case!

SPECIAL NOTE: *Educators are particularly fond of notes from home. In-deed, we know very few teachers who don't have at least one gem they remember from their careers. These could be used as is, or as parts of various speeches to make or illustrate your points.*

55

TOPICS:
Speaking out; problems; looking for solutions

AUDIENCE:
Suitable for all adult audiences and older students

When the child enrolled in school, his mother informed the authorities that there was a serious problem. The child did not speak. Consequently, the school set about an extensive series of tests on the child.

At the conclusion of these tests, two things were determined. The first was that there was no physical reason why this child could not talk. The second was that, try as they might, no one could get the child to utter a single word.

The school psychologist suggested that they place the child in a regular classroom in hopes that his peers could elicit from him what adults could not.

The boy made a fine adjustment to school and socialized regularly with his classmates, but, at the end of the first year, he still had not uttered a word.

So it went throughout the boy's school career. While he did not speak, his grades in school were outstanding, and the papers he handed in were intelligent and perceptive. His teachers liked him. The other students liked him. The only drawback was that he never spoke.

One other peculiarity about the child was his eating pattern at lunch. Every day, he would go to the cafeteria and order a chocolate milk and a hot dog. It was the same every school day of his life.

Finally, the boy reached his senior year of high school, and school authorities redoubled their efforts, determined to get this young man to speak before he left school for good. Try as they might, however, the year progressed with no sound from the student.

Then, one day in late May, the boy went to the cafeteria for lunch and got his chocolate milk and hot dog. Sitting at a table, he took one bite of his lunch, spit it out rather unceremoniously, and declared to the entire cafeteria, "This is the worst hot dog I have ever tasted!"

Immediately, he was surrounded by the specialists.

"What did you say?" said the principal.

"Say it again!" shouted the guidance counselor.

"Please repeat that!" echoed the school psychologist.

"I said," the boy repeated in a deep baritone voice, "that this is the worst hot dog I have ever tasted!"

"So, you *can* talk," the psychologist gasped. "Please, don't stop now. Why. . .why haven't you talked before now?"

"Well," said the boy, rather embarrassed by all the attention, "up until now, the hot dogs have always tasted great!"

SPECIAL NOTE: *It is easy to sit back and say nothing, but there comes a time when every person has to speak out and make his position known. We recommend that this story be used as an introduction to a speech centering on that theme.*

56

TOPICS:
Clever answers; student-teacher interaction

AUDIENCE:
Suitable for all audiences

In science class, the teacher was demonstrating how to grind a lens, and he remarked that optical companies had machines to do this task.

"You must be careful, however," the teacher continued, "that you don't get too close when they're in operation. Can you imagine what would happen if you fell into one of those lens grinding machines?"

"Yes," answered one clever young scientist, "you'd really make a spectacle of yourself!"

*   *   *

"What's the matter?" the young man asked his downtrodden friend.

"Well," sighed the other boy, "this afternoon our teacher told us that tomorrow we are going to study syntax."

"That doesn't surprise me," the first lad commented. "My father says they're taxing *everything* nowadays!"

*   *   *

"Bobby," asked the teacher, "what is an oyster?"
"An oyster," answered Bobby, "is a fish that's built like a nut!"

*   *   *

"One day my mom told me and my sister, Ruth, to go to the store for her," wrote the young boy in his composition. "We decided to take my bike. I pedaled, and Ruth rode behind me. On the way to the supermarket, I coasted down this huge hill. At the bottom there was this big pothole in the road. We hit the pothole, and I proceeded Ruthlessly with my task"

*   *   *

"And, after creating all the creatures of the earth," the Sunday School teacher told the class, "God told them to go forth and multiply."

"I'll bet these snakes in this book I got from the library didn't go forth and multiply," said one young man.

"How can you say that?" demanded the Sunday School teacher.

"Because, it says right here," the lad indicated, "that these snakes are adders!"

SPECIAL NOTE: These are rather short, but they can be used to advantage in any presentation or just to lighten the atmosphere at parent-teacher gatherings and the like.

57

TOPICS:
Short subjects; student-parent-teacher interaction; perspectives of children

AUDIENCE:
Suitable for all adult audiences, particularly parents

After dinner, young Alice went to her room to do her homework. Presently, there was a knock on the door, and her father entered and sat down next to her.

"Alice," he said, "I want to apologize to you. You know I've had a lot of work at the office recently, and I realize that for the past month, I've had to work in my study and haven't had time to help you with your homework.

"You'll be glad to know, however, that I'm all caught up on my work from the office, so tonight I want to help you with whatever homework you have!"

At which point, Alice began to sob quite loudly. Tenderly, her father put his arm around her.

"Oh, Alice," he said, "did you think I didn't love you, because I wasn't helping you with your homework?"

"Of course not," whimpered Alice.

"Then, what?" asked her father.

"It's just that . . ." sobbed Alice, "Well . . . it's just that since you *stopped* helping me with my homework, I've begun passing, and I was so looking forward to keeping my grades up!"

*   *   *

LETTER FROM SCHOOLBOY TO SCHOOLGIRL

Dear Annie,

I love you! I love you! I love you! I would do anything for you. I will fight the meanest kid in school if you want me to. I would walk through fire or swim the Atlantic Ocean for you. I am strong and brave and I am yours.

> Love,
> Harold

P.S. I will come to visit you tonight if my mommie lets me go out after dark.

*   *   *

"I'll make you a deal," said the teacher to the assembled parents of her students. "If you promise not to believe what your kids tell you about me, I promise not to believe what they tell me about you!"

*   *   *

Mother was reading to her daughter from the Bible.

"'Dust thou art,'" she quoted, "'and unto dust thou shalt return.'"

"Do you mean," asked her daughter, "that we either start out or end up as dust?"

"That's right," answered the mother.

"Then you'd better come up to my room," exclaimed the child, "because there's somebody under my bed who's either coming or going!"

*   *   *

"Now," said the math teacher, "suppose you had an apple pie that was cut into six pieces, and I asked you for two of them. How many pieces would you have left?"

One little girl vigorously waved her hand and was called on.

"I'd have six left," she told the teacher, "because I wouldn't give you none!"

*   *   *

Billy sat at the dining room table doing his homework. He had just begun to do some writing, when his pencil slipped and tore a hole in the paper. Angrily, he crumpled the paper into a ball which he flung across the room.

"Lousy paper!" he exclaimed as he began again.

No sooner had he started again than the point on his pencil

broke. This time, Billy broke the pencil in two, slammed it down on the table and roared, "Rotten, cheap pencil!"

He took out another pencil, but before he could get started, a breeze came through the window and blew the paper off the table.

"Why can't we get a decent table where things stay put!" he screamed at the top of his lungs as he stood up and gave a vicious kick to one leg of the table.

At this point, Tommy's mother came into the room.

"That will be enough of that, young man!" she stated, and, hoping to calm him down by changing the subject, she asked, "Just what are you writing about, anyway?"

"It's a 500-word composition," pouted the sullen lad, "on 'How I Learned to Control My Temper!'"

SPECIAL NOTE: *These short anecdotes reflect the often amusing interactions between parent and child and teacher and child that grow more humorous and treasured with the passing years. We have found that both parents and educators are very receptive to these stories.*

Afterthoughts

It has been said that the reason people laugh at stories about the blunders and mistakes of others is because it makes them feel superior. We're not too sure about that. While we don't deny that some may laugh for that reason, it has been our experience with teachers and parents that they laugh because they see themselves at that age in the children they teach and raise. They see the openness, the beginnings of knowledge, the trial and error involved in growing from a child to an adult. They see the struggle, the failure and the success, and their hearts fill with joy.

As educators, we can accept no other premise—if we look for the laughter, it will be there. If we see in the mistakes and errors of our children the vital process of growth and development, then we can approach them with the gentleness and understanding that they need. This will carry them over the rough spots and help them develop into adults who can laugh with and help their children.

It is a goal well worth pursuing!

Part 5
It's the "Principal" of the Thing

For a number of reasons, the principal of a modern school does not have an enviable or quiet position. There are factions, from the board of education through parents groups through professional education associations, that must be dealt with on an almost daily basis; there are budgets and meetings and public relations; there are a hundred daily tasks to do. Yet, this person remains in the place where, as Harry Truman said, "the buck stops!" He or she is responsible for the school—both the physical plant and the education that goes on inside.

Most educators realize this, and we have seen few schools where there has not been a good working relationship between the faculty and the principal. Indeed, we all realize that a principal can set the tenor and pace of a school and often make the difference between a place that is a joy to be in and a place where the day drags on.

Most principals we know have a well-developed sense of humor. As one of them told us, "You have to—otherwise you'd cry a lot!" The stories in this section concern principals and administrators of all kinds. Some stories were contributed by them; all were chosen to bring a smile to their lips. These selections are ideal for faculty gatherings, staff dinners, or any assembly where the school administrators are gathered.

You will find it is the principal who laughs loudest of all!

58

TOPICS:
School administrator; the difficulty of the particular
job

AUDIENCE:
Adults; particularly a group of school administrators

A small, traveling circus had set up its tents on the outskirts of town. The time for the evening performance was approaching, and the local townspeople were filling the big top.

Suddenly, one of the clowns in the show rushed up to the ringmaster waiving his hands frantically.

"It's Jocko!" the agitated clown exclaimed. "They've just taken him away in the ambulance! The doctor says it's his appendix. He has to be operated on immediately!"

"Oh, no!" sighed the ringmaster. "Without Jocko we have no show. He was our feature attraction. What are we going to do?"

Just then, a man stepped out of the line of people purchasing tickets for the show and walked up to the ringmaster.

"Pardon me," said the man, "but I couldn't help overhearing. You were talking about Jocko the Juggler. Well, if you need help, perhaps I could fill in for him?"

The ringmaster was a bit suspicious of this offer, but, since it was rapidly nearing show time, he accepted the man's offer and hastened him off to get into costume for the show.

When it came time for Jocko the Juggler to perform, the stranger stepped into the spotlight—and what a performance he gave! He juggled everything in sight, and he did it flawlessly. At one point, the man had ten objects in the air at the same time, and he never missed a single one! He was, in fact, better than Jocko had ever been.

After the show, the ringmaster came backstage to where the stranger was changing back into his regular clothes.

"You were fantastic," said the ringmaster. "How would you like a regular job with us? I'll hire you right now."

"Oh, I'm sorry," said the man, "but I couldn't do that. I already have a job. My name is Ed Jones, and I'm the principal of the local high school. The only reason I came forward at all is that—considering what I do all day—I figured that juggling hoops and plates and balls ought to be a snap!"

SPECIAL NOTE: *This story goes over very well with any group of administrators, as it implies the difficulty of their job as well as the ease with which they handle so many, complex matters each day. Of course, the position as "principal" could be changed to "superintendent" or any other administrative job, and the name used could be that of a local principal with the actual school name substituted for "the local high school."*

Stories about the difficulty of a particular job always go over well.

59

TOPICS:
Vice-principal; working difficulties; how children view work

AUDIENCE:
Suitable for all adult audiences, particularly administrators

At first, Harry's mother was concerned about taking the position of vice-principal at the same school her son attended. Upon consideration, however, she came to the conclusion that it might do her son some good to see exactly what his mother did on the job.

What she did not expect, was the deluge of work that awaited her as vice-principal. Sometimes it seemed as if every problem in the world had been dumped in her lap. Each matter required immediate attention, and it seemed that she barely entered her office before the telephone rang or the secretary dumped a huge pile of papers on her desk.

September passed, and on the first day of October, the woman realized that she had barely been out of her office for the entire time. She threw down her pen and walked out into the hallway.

Lunch had just started in the cafeteria, and she walked up to the first table of children she saw and began talking to them. Soon she was laughing and joking with the children, thoroughly enjoying herself, and she even shared a cookie one of the children offered her. As she rose to leave to get back to her work, she noticed that her son was in that lunch period, staring at her from another table.

The rest of the day was particularly long, and, by the time she got home, she was exhausted. She had just taken off her shoes and was relaxing on the sofa, when her son bounced into the room.

"Hey, Mom!" he shouted, "how about going outside and throwing a ball around?"

"Harry," she said imploringly, "can it wait until after dinner? I've had a rough day. You have no idea how difficult it is being the vice-principal."

"What do you mean," said Harry. "It's not hard. I been there a month, and all I ever seen you do is party with the sixth-graders and steal their cookies!"

SPECIAL NOTE: *Of course, you might substitute the name of a newly appointed vice-principal in your district, or make it any other administrative job. This is also a good story for pointing out how children, and sometimes others as well, may not recognize the difficulties inherent in a particular task or job.*

60

TOPICS:
Principal; natural intelligence; finding our way

AUDIENCE:
Suitable for all adult audiences

The principal was late for a meeting on the other side of town, and because he was rushing, he made a wrong turn and ended up in a section of the city with which he was not familiar. He was totally and completely lost.

As he searched desperately for signs, he happened to notice a boy standing on the corner and recognized him as a student from his school.

"Barry!" the principal shouted as he pulled up to the curb. "How do I get to Bell Avenue from here?"

"Gosh, Mr. Jones," answered the lad, "I don't know."

All right, then just tell me how to get to Main Street. I'll know the way from there."

"I don't know how to get to Main Street, Mr. Jones," said the boy.

"Well, then, tell me how to get to River Drive!"

"I don't know how to get there either," the lad said.

Becoming more and more frustrated and losing his patience, the principal blurted, "You don't know much of anything do you, Barry?"

"I guess not," said Barry with a smile, "but, then again, Mr. Jones, I ain't the one who's lost!"

SPECIAL NOTE: These little stories where people get their "comeuppance" seem to go over well with almost any group. Again, do not fear to personalize this story by substituting the name of the administrator of your school or district for the one in the story. Doing this ensures that it will get a big laugh.

61

TOPICS:
Discipline; principal; ambiguous questions

AUDIENCE:
Suitable for all adult audiences

It had been a particularly rough day for the principal, and he was looking forward to going home when the door to his office opened and in walked the gym teacher accompanied by one of the students. From the looks on their faces, the principal knew that this was a disciplinary case.

After getting the details and when he was finally alone with the student, the principal knew he recognized the boy. Getting the boy's file, he found that the youngster had, indeed, been sent to the office for disciplinary reasons five times previously.

"Young man," bellowed the principal, "you've been up before me in the past, haven't you?"

"I don't think so," answered the boy.

"How can you say that?" the principal asked, brandishing the student's record. 'You *have* been up before me!"

"Honest, Mr. Jones," the youngster protested, "I haven't. Why, I don't even know what time you get up!"

SPECIAL NOTE: This is one of those "silly" stories that gets a good response nevertheless. While the man in the story is a principal, this story could be equally adapted to another position such as guidance counselor, coach, et cetera.

62

TOPICS:
Children; discipline; parents and the school

AUDIENCE:
Suitable for all adult audiences, particularly parents

"Pop," said the boy, "do you think that kids should be punished?"

"Well, Son," answered the father, putting down his paper, "that's a hard one to answer. Sometimes, a punishment can help a youngster think about what he's doing and correct a wrong action, especially if the child has done something very bad . . ."

"If he's done something bad," the boy interrupted. "But, what if a kid did nothing? Should he be punished then?"

"Of course not, Son," said the father. "To punish anybody for doing nothing is wrong. Why, only the meanest and most cruel kind of person would punish a child for doing nothing."

"I'm so glad to hear you say that," sighed the lad, "because for the last month I didn't do my homework, and I didn't do two book reports, and now the principal wants to keep me after school. Why don't you call her up right now and tell her what a terrible person she is!"

SPECIAL NOTE: This is a good story to use when there are parents in attendance as well as the administrator. It involves both and can be used just to get a laugh or to begin an investigation of problems in which both the home and the school are involved.

63

TOPICS:
Children's views; principal; misunderstanding

AUDIENCE:
Suitable for adult audiences and older students

The principal of the school was new to the job and instituted a great many changes when he took charge. He was a bundle of energy, and he made himself quite visible in the halls and classrooms of the building.

He also had quite a flair for the dramatic and held a number of assemblies in which he took an active part.

One day in February, just before Lincoln's birthday, he called an assembly. When all the students had been seated, the lights dimmed and the curtain parted to reveal the new principal standing in the center of the stage dressed as Abraham Lincoln.

He wore a top hat, a frock coat and striped pants, and he sported a magnificent false beard. He was the very image of old Abe.

The audience was stunned. Then, suddenly, one child leaned over to another, and, in a stage whisper that could be heard throughout the hall, said, "I knew it! This guy ain't gonna be satisfied until somebody shoots him!"

SPECIAL NOTE: *This always gets a big laugh, particularly if the administrator who is present is known to be a rather dynamic figure. It might also be used to point out that children do not always have the perception to recognize efforts in their behalf.*

64

TOPICS:
Short subjects; principal; discipline; getting caught in words

AUDIENCE:
Suitable for all audiences

The principal was in his office when he received a long-distance call from a supply house from which the school had ordered several items. The caller informed the principal that there was a problem in shipping the materials, and the principal began to explain rather forcefully that the school needed the supplies without delay.

The conversation grew very loud and heated just as one of the teachers walked into the main office.

"What's happening?" he inquired of the secretary.

"Hush!" she said. "Mr. Jones is talking to Los Angeles!"

"Well," remarked the teacher, "I really think it would be easier if he used a telephone."

*   *   *

The teacher had developed a bad case of laryngitis, and it was virtually impossible, and quite painful, for him to continue with classes. Consequently, he came to the main office to inform the principal that he was leaving to go to the doctor's.

When the teacher entered, the only person present was a student who was acting as office aide. The teacher motioned the student over, swallowed hard, grimaced in pain, and leaned close to the girl.

"Is the principal in?" he whispered with a pained expression on his face.

"Yes," the student whispered back with a furtive glance toward the principal's closed door, "but I don't think he's heard you yet. You can still get away!"

SPECIAL NOTE: *These are short anecdotes that view the principal in a not-altogether-favorable light. If said with a smile, however, everyone will understand the intention of the humor.*

65

TOPICS:

Wet paint; principal and students; a child's sense of humor

AUDIENCE:

Suitable for all audiences

It was a fine spring day, and the principal of the school decided to take a walk around the grounds. He ended his journey at the playground area and sat down on a bench to enjoy the warm and beautiful day.

Just then a little second grade boy came over and stood directly in front of him.

"Son," said the principal, "I see your classmates playing out on the field. Why don't you go out and join them?"

"I don't wanna," said the youngster.

The principal shifted uneasily on the bench and tried again.

"Growing boys and girls need to play," he stated, "so go ahead and join your classmates."

"I'd rather stay here," said the boy.

"And why do you want to stay here?" the principal asked rather forcefully.

"To watch you get up," the boy stated flatly. "The custodian just painted that bench ten minutes ago!"

SPECIAL NOTE: This incident actually happened to a friend of ours. It is another example of the kind of incident that is upsetting when it happens, but that is fondly told and retold for many years afterward.

66

TOPICS:
Roughing it; love of comfort; modern conveniences

AUDIENCES:
Suitable for all audiences

The principal of the school began a campaign of physical fitness in the building. He organized exercise groups among the faculty. He thought up a program of intramural sports. He even organized a hiking club composed of several of the older students.

Finally, he organized a weekend trip to a nearby nature preserve.

"On this trip," he told his wife, "we are going to live primitively, close to nature. We'll eat only what we can catch. We'll walk up mountains; we'll sleep on the hard ground. We'll live like the pioneers!"

"Really," said his wife. "Well, can I do anything to help?"

"Definitely!" said the principal. "Tonight I want you to turn the electric blanket down to the lowest setting so I can be in shape by Saturday!"

SPECIAL NOTE: With the growing interest in physical fitness, this story is a natural. It can lead to a talk about the physical education program, recreational activities, or any one of the sports programs in a school.

67

TOPICS:
Embarrassment; alcohol; compromising situations

AUDIENCE:
Suitable for all adult audiences

As part of a program entitled Early Awareness of Alcohol and Drug Abuse, the principal sent out notices inviting every family to a meeting on alcohol abuse. The notice also proclaimed that several children would participate in the program.

Since Billy was one of the participants, his mother and father came early and had a chance to speak with the principal.

"We're trying to teach children the dangers of starting to drink at an early age," the principal told the parents. "Billy is going to act out a little scene where I try to get him to take a drink and he refuses."

When that part of the program came, Billy's parents were beaming with pride.

"Billy," said the principal in a loud stage voice, "how would you like a little glass of wine?"

"No, thank you, sir," Billy recited loudly.

"Oh, do have some wine. It can't hurt you."

"No, sir, I won't," came Billy's memorized response. "I do not want to abuse myself with alcohol!"

With that, the principal smiled, and the parents applauded.

"That was very good, Billy," said the principal. "Now, I'd like to depart from the script for a moment and ask Billy what he would do if someone really did offer him a glass of wine."

"I'd say *no*, just like my daddy does," Billy answered honestly.

"Marvelous!" the principal exclaimed. "Your father doesn't drink wine?"

"No, sir. And, if somebody offered me wine, I'd say the same thing my daddy does."

The principal was glowing with joy.

"And what is that, my boy? Please tell us."

"I'd say, 'Thank you very much, but I do not like to drink wine . . .' " And Billy paused, as if remembering. Then his eyes grew bright, and he continued, " 'but if it's all the same to you, I *will* have an extra dry martini, straight up, with a twist!' "

SPECIAL NOTE: *This story could be used effectively to launch a program on substance abuse. It might also be used to point out that we teach by example as well as by words.*

68

TOPICS:
Quick thinking; justice; being cheated

AUDIENCE:
Suitable for adult audiences and older students

The principal from the Midwest came East for the first time to attend a conference in New York City. He arrived at La Guardia airport and immediately went outside to hail a taxi.

He gave the driver the name of his hotel and arrived there after a seventy-five minute drive to find that he had run up an enormous cab fare. Grudgingly, he paid the tariff and went to his room.

He was recounting this story to someone he met at the conference, when the fellow stopped him.

"You've been taken," the man said. "Most cabbies are fine, but every now and then, you find someone unscrupulous who will drive a visitor around for a while and take a much longer route than necessary in order to pad the bill!"

The conference ended, and it was time for the principal to return home. He got his luggage and hailed a cab in front of the hotel.

"La Guardia please, driver," the principal said.

They took off, and after about twenty minutes of driving, the principal realized that he was being cheated again. He said nothing, however, but relaxed and enjoyed the sights of the city.

An hour and thirty minutes later, they pulled up at the terminal. The principal leaped from the taxi and immediately motioned a policeman to the cab.

"Officer," the principal said, "how much would you say a cab fare should be from the Billings Hotel to La Guardia?"

The officer told him, and the principal dug in his pocket and extracted that amount.

Handing the money to the officer, he said, "Would you be kind enough to pay the driver for me. I'm afraid I'm very late for my plane!"

And with a smile to the driver, the principal darted into the building.

SPECIAL NOTE: *This story goes over very well, particularly with any group from a large city. While not common, thankfully, incidents such as the one in the story do happen, and everyone enjoys the inherent justice and triumph of the underdog.*

69

TOPICS:
Guests; husband-wife relationships; embarrassment

AUDIENCE:
Suitable for all adult audiences

"Guess what," the principal told his wife, "I was talking with the superintendent today and found out that we both love clams casino. I invited him over for dinner tonight so he could try yours."

"You did what?" his wife exploded. "How could you? It's too late now to get to the store, and I only have a dozen clams. Promise me you won't eat any more than four of them."

The principal promised, and his wife prepared the delicacy.

When the superintendent arrived and dinner had begun, the clams were quickly gone. The principal, seemingly forgetting the earlier conversation with his wife, asked the superintendent if he would like another serving.

His wife frowned deeply, but the superintendent declined with thanks. Again, however, the principal insisted that the guest have another helping. Again the wife grimaced, and again the superintendent refused politely. A third time the principal insisted that the man have more. This time his wife gritted her teeth, and the superintendent firmly declined the offer.

Somehow, they got through the rest of the evening. When the superintendent left, the principal's wife turned on him furiously.

"Why, in heaven's name, did you insist that he have more clams?" shouted the wife. "I told you we didn't have any more!"

"I'm sorry!" exclaimed the principal. "I completely forgot!"

"You forgot? Then why did you think I was kicking you under the table each time you asked him to have more?"

"Kicking me?" said the principal with an amazed expression on his face. "You never kicked me."

SPECIAL NOTE: *This is an amusing story to tell if you happen to have a local principal and superintendent in the same audience. You would use their names, of course, to make it more relevant.*

70

TOPICS:
Promotion; mistaken communication; children's
perspective; administrators

AUDIENCE:
Suitable for adult audiences and older students

The little third-grader arrived at the main office in tears and
demanded to see the principal at once. The principal, who happened
to be standing by her door, overheard the child and asked the little
girl to step into her office.

When the child was seated and had composed herself, she
looked at the principal and asked, "Mrs. Jones, are you gonna stop
being our principal and become the superintendent of schools?"

"Jane," Mrs. Jones answered quietly, "I didn't think anybody
knew about it yet, but yes, I am going to become superintendent."

The little girl drew a deep breath and began crying all over again.

"There, there, Jane," soothed Mrs. Jones, "I won't be leaving
you. I'll still be around and visit the school and your class."

"It's not that," sobbed Jane. "I like you, and I don't want you
to get hurt."

"Hurt, whatever do you mean?"

"Well," continued Jane, "I heard my teacher talking to the
fourth grade teacher, and she said, 'It looks as if they're finally going
to take old Jonesy and kick her upstairs.'

"I just hope it isn't gonna hurt too much!"

*SPECIAL NOTE: Children often see situations quite differently than we
do as adults. Use the name of your local superintendent
or principal, especially on the occasion of such a promotion, and this story will go over well.*

71

TOPICS:
Faculty meetings; boring speeches; teacher-principal interaction

AUDIENCE:
Suitable for all adult audiences, particularly educators

A faculty meeting at which the principal of the school was to speak had been scheduled for that afternoon, and word spread that the superintendent of schools was coming to sit in on the gathering.

One of the teachers was getting a drink of water in the hall prior to entering the library where the faculty meeting was to be held, when he noticed the superintendent coming down the hall.

The superintendent looked terrible! His face was sallow and sunken, he walked in a listless manner, there were huge black circles under his eyes, and virtually all life seemed to have been drained from him.

"Sir," said the teacher in the hall, "if you don't mind my saying so, you don't look good. Is anything wrong?"

"Oh, I'm all right," answered the superintendent. "I suffer from insomnia, and I haven't been able to get to sleep for the past week. I'd give anything to sleep, but nothing I've done seems to help."

"Sir," said the teacher as he guided the superintendent toward the meeting in the library, "come with me. Have I got a cure for you!"

SPECIAL NOTE: *While faculty meetings may be a necessary part of teaching, they can become long and drawn out, as any educator will attest. Therefore, this story goes over very well with all educators. We heard this story used as an introduction to a discussion on how to improve in-service sessions. It went along the lines of, "We all agree that these meetings can be long and fruitless, so how can we make them meaningful and productive . . . ?"*

72

TOPICS:
Principal and PTA; quick stories; misunderstanding

AUDIENCE:
Suitable for all adult audiences

The principal was addressing the PTA at a school night function with the entire faculty present.

"I wonder," said the principal, "if each parent could please stand up and give the name of his or her child. The faculty has informed me that they are quite anxious to get you tied up with your child!"

* * *

The mother and father couldn't find a sitter for the evening, so they came to the PTA meeting with their six-month-old baby. The place was crowded, and they got separated, finally ending up on opposite ends of a row.

Toward the end of the meeting, the father, who was holding the baby, fished into his pocket for a scrap of paper, feverishly wrote a note, and handed it to a teacher who was standing nearby. Father pointed to the note and then to the other end of the row indicating his wife.

The teacher, however, misunderstood and thought the note was for the principal who was also sitting toward the end of the row. Therefore, he delivered the note to the principal.

About the time the note arrived, the principal was called up to the stage to make some announcements, and he merely placed the note with the other papers he was carrying.

The principal got up to the platform, cleared his throat, and began to read from his notes.

"There will be a bake sale this Saturday at the game," he announced. "The PTA executive board will meet Thursday evening at 7:30. And, where the hell did you put the diaper; this kid is soaking wet!"

* * *

It was the holiday get-together of the PTA, and it was going very well. Both parents and the faculty seemed to be having a good time, and everyone was in high spirits.

The president of the PTA checked her watch and approached the principal.

"Everybody seems to be having a great time," she said. "Shall we let them enjoy themselves a little longer, or do you want to give your speech now?"

*   *   *

The president of the PTA invited the school principal and his wife to dine with her and her husband. When the guests arrived, the door was opened by the seven-year-old son of the hosts.

"Mister," said the boy, "are you a famous actor?"

"Actor?" said the principal. "No, I'm not, but why do you ask?"

"Well," said the lad, "when Mommy told Daddy that you were coming to dinner, Daddy said that if you came, there was bound to be a big scene!"

SPECIAL NOTE: *Since these stories revolve around the principal and the PTA, they are best used at any occasion where that group may be meeting. They also go over well with any group of parents.*

Afterthoughts

While all the stories in this section revolve around the principal or some other administrator, there is no reason why they cannot be adapted to a teacher or any other individual as the central character.

Many of these stories poke fun at the administrator, and, while they are generally well-received and everyone knows they are just in fun, it is always a good idea to thank the administrator for being such a good sport when you are finished. In that way, you clear up even the slightest doubt that there may be any enmity between you and the principal. You may think this a small point, indeed, but all you need is to have one person misunderstand and the situation could become sensitive.

Told with a smile and a gleam in the eye, however, these stories will make for an enjoyable time whenever they are told.

Part 6

Where Do the Teachers Sleep?

L ooking back at childhood memories, we can remember being absolutely amazed the first time we saw a teacher outside of school. If that teacher happened to have a husband and children with her, it was totally eye-opening. You mean that the teachers *don't* live at the school? They actually have homes and families, just like *real* people? Indeed, we actually know of one pre-kindergarten youngster who was being given a tour of the school prior to entry and was asked if he had any questions. He had only one: "Where do the teachers sleep?"

As educators, we are aware that children view us differently than they do their parents or relatives or even their next-door neighbor. For many, perhaps even the majority of them, the only time they see us is at school. We are there when they arrive in the morning and there when they leave in the afternoon. In their minds, we are intrinsically tied up with the school itself, and a great many elementary educators have told us that many children actually believe that teachers live in the school.

In this section, we will be looking at stories that reflect a child's view of school life. We'll look into the classroom, into teacher-student relationships, into parents and teachers—all as seen through the eyes of the children. We will be looking at children's perceptions of teachers.

The results are often hilarious.

73

TOPICS:
Rumors; children's perceptions; embarrassment

AUDIENCE:
Suitable for all adult audiences

"Oh," said the principal's secretary, "I just got something in my eye! Oh, that smarts!"

"Try rubbing it toward your nose," commented the principal. "That always works for me."

After a few minutes and several home remedies, the eye was no better.

"This is really starting to bother me," the secretary complained.

"There's only one thing to do," offered the principal. "I'll lift up your eyelid and take out the cinder with the edge of my handkerchief. There's nothing to worry about; I do this for my kids all the time."

With that, the principal took out a clean, white handkerchief and drew the end of it to a point. Coming around his desk, he placed one hand along the secretary's cheek and lifted the eyelid with the thumb of that hand. He bent over until he was about two inches from her face and began to study the eye intently.

"Be careful," cautioned the nervous secretary.

"Don't worry," soothed the principal. "I just want to get close enough to . . ."

At which point, the door to the principal's office flew open, and there stood an eighth-grade boy with a discipline referral sheet in his hand. The boy gazed for a moment, and then began to smile.

"I . . . I was just taking something out of Miss Smith's eye," said the principal as he straightened up. "You believe me, don't you?"

"Why, of course I believe you, sir," said the boy. "Miss Smith got something in her eye, and you were just taking it out. I believe you 100 percent, sir. Oh, and, sir?"

"Yes?"

"I just want you to know," continued the lad with a wink, "the moment we tear up this referral sheet, I'll swear to it!"

SPECIAL NOTE: Of such simple beginnings can far-reaching rumors be made. This is a good story for use with parents, pointing out to them that children often misconstrue what they see and hear, and that any rumors brought home should be checked out with you or the school. They get the point.

74

TOPICS:
Overwork; a student's perception

AUDIENCE:
Suitable for all audiences, particularly educators

Around the dinner table one evening, the father asked his son that time-honored question that parents have been asking their offspring probably from the time of Socrates: "What did you do in school today?"

The man's son gave the equally time-honored response: "Nothing," which translates to "Nothing I want to make the effort to tell you about right now."

"Come on," said the father, "you must have done something."

"Well," said the boy, "we did have a special science class today."

"That's more like it. What was so special about it?"

"Well, we all went down to the auditorium, and Mr. Jenkins, our science teacher, gave us a lecture about the circulatory system of the frog."

"And did that last all period?" father asked.

"All period?" answered the lad. "We were there for *two* periods. Mr. Jenkins lectured for an hour and forty-five minutes without a break!"

"An hour and forty-five minutes!" exclaimed the father. "Why the man must have been exhausted!"

"No, Mr. Jenkins was just fine," said his son, "but you should have seen the rest of the class!"

SPECIAL NOTE: Knowledge rarely comes without an expenditure of energy on the student's part. Sometimes that involves just listening. School is real WORK for the child who is striving to learn, and everyone, teachers and parents, should be aware of that fact. This story is a natural lead-in to a discussion along these or similar lines.

75

TOPICS:
Practical jokes; quick thinking; teacher-student interaction

AUDIENCE:
Suitable for adult audiences, particularly educators

A certain teacher in our school was extremely popular with his classes, and a great deal of comaraderie and good-natured teasing took place along with outstanding learning.

The students of one particular class decided to play a practical joke on their favorite teacher. They arranged with a student to delay the teacher's arrival in class. One student took a life-size model of a chimpanzee from the science office and placed it in the teacher's chair. Another student managed to get the teacher's hat from the faculty lounge and placed it on the chimp's head. A third student took the teacher's spare eyeglasses from the desk and placed these on the chimp as well. Then, they all settled back as if not a thing were wrong and awaited the teacher's arrival.

When the teacher walked through the door, there were many repressed giggles, but most students kept straight faces.

The teacher didn't say a word. Instead, he looked at the chimp, then at his class, and finally back at the chimp. Taking the hat from the chimp's head, he put it on and began to walk out the door.

"Mr. Smith!" yelled one student. "Please, don't be mad; it was only a joke!"

"Mad? Why I'm not mad at all," Mr. Smith replied. "I was just leaving, because I figured I wasn't needed anymore. In fact, I'm overjoyed that this class has finally gotten a teacher who is so ideally suited to their level of intelligence!"

SPECIAL NOTE: We have found that educators are particularly well-disposed to this story. Classes have played tricks on their teachers for centuries and probably will for centuries to come. When there is strong mutual respect, however, this can draw teacher and class even closer together and establish a firm foundation for learning.

76

TOPICS:
Quick thinking; student-teacher interaction; clever answers

AUDIENCE:
Well-suited for an audience of educators

The science teacher often used to conduct his experiments with his class in the basement of the school, mainly because it was a quiet area and the class would be undisturbed for the length of the experiments.

One day, the teacher was required to meet with a committee on which he was serving during the time when he would normally be conducting experiments.

Not wishing his class to miss an important part of their studies, he requested that a substitute teacher come in to supervise, and he placed his brightest pupil in charge of arranging and conducting the actual experiment.

The teacher had been in his committee meeting less than fifteen minutes when a student arrived at the door looking for him.

"Sir," said the student, "one of the pipes in the basement has started to leak."

"Shut off the valve that controls that pipe and get back to work" said the teacher.

Ten minutes went by and there was another knock on the door and another student from his class.

"We turned off the valve," said the student, "and the pipe stopped leaking, but now there's water coming from the valve, and the whole floor is wet."

"Hasn't the study of science taught you anything?" chided the teacher. "Go back there, study the problem, use your ingenuity, and don't bother me again!"

Five minutes later, however, the student was back at the door, his trousers wet to the knees.

"Sir," said the boy, "we tried everything, and it just won't stop."

"Then try something else," the exasperated teacher moaned.

"But, sir, it's flooding! What should we do?"

Placing one hand on the boy's shoulder, the teacher gazed serenely into the student's eyes and said, "Rise above it, young man; rise above it!"

SPECIAL NOTE: *This is a story for educators. We have found that they generally enjoy this. The quick thinking of the person in the story is appreciated, especially since there are so many times in an educator's day when quick thinking is exactly what is called for.*

77

TOPICS:
Kindergarten; tact; embarrassment; children and the truth

AUDIENCE:
Suitable for all adult audiences

The precocious kindergarten tot was ready for her first day of school, and Mother dutifully brought her to the assigned classroom to meet her teacher.

When they arrived, they found the teacher waiting for them. The woman was very pleasant and gentle with the children, but she was also extremely large. Indeed, she must have weighed well over two hundred and fifty pounds.

The youngster stared at the massive woman, and her small mouth hung open in wonder. Suddenly she began to tug insistently on her mother's hand.

"What is it, dear?" asked her mother. "What's the matter?"

Just then, as the large kindergarten teacher came forward to greet them, the child said, in the loudest stage whisper imaginable, "F-A-T, ain't she, Ma?"

SPECIAL NOTE: Sometimes, children can be honest with a brutality that is frightening. This story invariably causes a chuckle, because it strikes so true.

78

TOPICS:
Honesty; frankness; classroom "boners" between teacher and student

AUDIENCE:
Suitable for all adult audiences

"Harry," said the teacher, "I want to talk to you. For the first month of school, your homework was just perfect, with everything done correctly. Now, for the past week, there has been nothing but little mistakes all over your papers. How do you account for that?"

"Modern technology," sighed Harry.

"What do you mean, 'modern technology'?" the teacher asked.

"Well," said Harry, "last week my mother got a brand new microwave oven, so now she has time to help me with my homework!"

*　　*　　*

It was time for the first report card of the new school year, and the children waited anxiously as the teacher passed them out. Most of the children studied the cards, sighed, and looked either very happy or very sad. All, that is, except for one girl whose face grew red with anger as she stomped to the teacher's desk.

"Karen?" asked the teacher. "What's wrong?"

"Mr. Jones, this is very unfair. You can't do this!"

"What do you mean?" said the teacher. "As I recall, you received very good marks."

"You call this good!" Karen exclaimed as she pointed to the report card. "You gave me an "F" in Sex, and you never even told us we were supposed to study it!"

*　　*　　*

The teacher was trying to teach her energetic young class about occupations, not only the various types of occupations, but the duties and salaries attendant to each.

The morning had not gone well, and the teacher had spent considerable time just getting the class settled and working. It seemed they no sooner quieted down, than some new outbreak of high spirits occurred that required the teacher's attention.

Finally, they seemed ready, and the teacher began her lesson on occupations. She began with the teaching profession, figuring that it was an occupation with which the children would be familiar. She began by seeing if the children had any idea of a teacher's salary.

"Mary," she asked a student, "what would you accept to teach this class?"

Mary's eyes widened.

"Little devils like us?" said the child. "Forget it, Miss Wilson, you don't *have* that much!"

*   *   *

The teacher stood before her second grade class.

"Boys and girls," she said. "Many of you know that at the beginning of last year, when you were starting first grade, I was Miss Jones. Then, in the middle of that year, I got married and became Mrs. Smith.

"Well, class, in a few weeks, I'm going to be leaving this school. I'll miss you, but I'm going to wait for a bundle of joy of my own!"

The children looked at each other with puzzled eyes.

Sensing that they had not understood, the teacher continued, "You know, there's going to be a blessed event for my husband and me."

Again, the children scratched their heads and raised their eyebrows questioningly.

"A little package from heaven!" the teacher tried desperately.

One little girl stood up in the back of the room.

"Mrs. Smith," she stated flatly, "you're not trying to tell us you're pregnant, are you?"

SPECIAL NOTE: *These are stories with a great deal of audience appeal. They never fail to get a big response whether the audience be composed primarily of parents or educators.*

79

TOPICS:
Insensitivity; a child's view of tragedy; differing perceptions

AUDIENCE:
Suitable for all adult audiences

In history class, the teacher was telling her students about Mount Vesuvius and the famous eruption that buried Pompeii. She wanted to make history as vivid as possible for her class, so, using all her knowledge of the tragedy, she began to describe the horrible event as graphically as she could.

"You must picture it, children," she began. "Hundreds of people running through the streets in fear and panic! Red-hot lava pouring down the hillside! Burning ash falling on the fear-stricken people from the sky! Horrible gases choking them at every turn! It was horrible, children, horrible!"

"Miss Jones," said a child from the rear.

"Yes, Mary."

"Gosh, Miss Jones," said the young girl, "if it was that bad, why didn't they just change the channel?"

SPECIAL NOTE: Perhaps it is the release of tension after the very serious story within the story, but this anecdote gets tremendous laughs. It also points out the fact that children are often far removed from the seriousness of a situation, a fact we should all recognize.

80

TOPICS:
Laziness; student perceptions of teachers; misunderstanding

AUDIENCE:
Suitable for adult audiences, particularly educators

Father was trying to instruct his son in the finer moral virtues.

"Above all, Son," the man said, "you must work hard and never be lazy."

"What do you mean by 'lazy,' Dad?" the boy asked.

"Well, Son," he answered, "just think of your class in school. Surely there must be someone in your class who is lazy. For example, when the class is busy studying or writing, isn't there someone who just sits back and watches the rest of you at work but does nothing himself? Someone who lets the rest of you work while he or she just watches?"

"Now I understand!" said the boy. "You mean the teacher!"

SPECIAL NOTE: You know, if you asked most elementary schoolchildren, we don't think one in ten would conceive of teaching as a "job" any more than they consider the tasks done by their mothers as "work." Teachers, like mothers, are simply "there." In a reverse sort of way, this anecdote brings out the point that teaching is, indeed, a difficult task requiring hard work. This is an ideal lead-in for a speech to parents or the general public emphasizing the importance of the teacher's work in society.

81

TOPICS:
Short subjects; student-teacher interaction; clever answers

AUDIENCE:
Suitable for all audiences

"At the time," the teacher told the class, "there was a saying that the sun never set on the British empire. Now, who can tell me what that means?"

Several hands went up, and the teacher called on one student.

"That means," he said, "that everyday, just before sunset, they would take down the flag and carry it inside!"

*   *   *

"You know something, Mom," said little Debbie, "I think my teacher is dumb!"

"Debbie!" exclaimed her mother, "how can you say something like that!"

"Well, it's true!" protested the child. "She doesn't even know what a rabbit is!"

"Come, now, Debbie, surely you must be mistaken."

"Nope!" Debbie continued. "Today I drew a picture of a rabbit with five ears and six eyes, and when the teacher looked at it, she said, 'Now, what do you suppose this is?'"

*   *   *

"Suppose," questioned the teacher, "that you made a product that cost you $1.98 to make and you sold it for $14.95. Further suppose that in your first year of manufacture, you sold 33,986 units. At the end of the year, what would you have?"

The boy thought for a moment and answered with a smile, "A red Trans-Am and a twenty-room house in the country!"

*   *   *

"Class," said the teacher, "I want you to write a composition of fifty words in length. It is to be about your pet. You can get started now."

The class began to write. In a few short minutes, however, one young man handed in his composition and claimed that it was completed.

"When I call my dog, Spot," read the composition, "I say 'Here, Spot; Here, Spot; Here, Spot; Here, Spot; Here, Spot; Here, Spot; Here, Spot; Here, Spot; Here, Spot; Here, Spot; Here, Spot; Here, Spot; Here, Spot; Here, Spot; Here, Spot; Here, Spot; Here, Spot; Here, Spot; Here, Spot' until he comes."

SPECIAL NOTE: *Here, again, we have several stories which go over well with both parents and educators. You might use some of them to illustrate that clear, firm direction is sometimes needed to get children to do their schoolwork.*

82

TOPICS:
Psychology; problems; adult views of children's behavior

AUDIENCE:
Suitable for parents and educators

The kindergarten teacher directed the class to draw a picture of a "happy" day. Most of the children drew flowers and trees and clouds and the sun in bright greens and blues and yellows.

All, that is, but little Billy. His picture was a study in somberness. A deep purple landscape was dotted with dark brown trees with purple leaves. Dark clouds of brown floated in a sky dominated by a black sun.

The teacher was somewhat taken aback by this stark rendering, and she called the home to find out if there was anything bothering Billy. The parents informed her that they were aware of no difficulty and that everything seemed to be going well at home.

When they saw the picture, however, the parents were equally upset by the somber tone and black sun, and they called the school and requested that the child study team meet with their son.

The child study team entered the classroom just as the children were handing in pictures they had drawn of a flower. Billy's flower had a brown stalk, purple leaves, and a black center. It was an ode to depression.

The team called in the school psychologist who talked with Billy for over an hour and reported that Billy seemed to be a normal six-year-old. There was no explanation for the somber drawings.

Finally, it was decided that the psychologist, the child study team, the teacher, and the parents should meet with Billy and talk this out. The next day found all of them in the psychologist's office.

"Billy," said the psychologist, "do you remember these drawings?"

"Sure," said Billy, "Miss Jones had us do them in class."

"That's right," said the teacher. "Well, Billy, we were just wondering why you drew these. I mean, all the other children drew green grass and leaves and blue sky and a yellow sun. How come the only colors you use are dark brown, deep purple, and black?"

"That's easy, Miss Jones," smiled Billy. "When you have us draw, you pass around that big box full of crayons. Well, I sit in the last seat in the last row, so by the time it gets to me, those are the only colors left!"

SPECIAL NOTE: *Let us not be too quick to impose our adult interpretations on children's behavior. This seems to be the moral we can learn from this story. And it's a worthwhile message to pass on to your audience. This ancedote also contains the message that we need to be very sure of our facts when dealing with children.*

83

TOPICS:
Vice and virtue; God; teachers; students and morality

AUDIENCE:
Suitable for all adult audiences

The teacher had an apple tree on her property which always put out a bumper crop. One Saturday, she happened to look out the window and saw two boys sneaking into her yard and heading for the tree.

Nabbing them red-apple-handed, so to speak, she did not chastise them, but rather invited them inside where she seated the boys at the kitchen table, cut up the applies, and poured each boy a large glass of milk.

When they had finished eating and drinking, the teacher looked at them and said, "Now, tell me, boys, wasn't that a whole lot better than sneaking in and stealing those apples?"

"Yes, ma'am," said one, "it sure was!"

"And do you know why that was?" asked the teacher.

"Sure," said the other. "If we had stolen them, we wouldn't have gotten the milk to drink!"

*   *   *

The teacher noticed an illustrated card on the desk of one of her students. Upon closer examination, it proved to be a scene of a fatherly figure in white robes and with a long white beard, seated in an idyllic pastoral setting, with children at his feet. At the bottom of the card was the inscription, "God is Love."

"Did you get this at church?" inquired the teacher.

"Yeah," said the child. "It's an advertisement for heaven."

*   *   *

"Class," said the Sunday School teacher, "today we are going to be talking about hymns. Mary, will you please tell me the name of your favorite hymn?"

Mary rose, her face blushing like a sunset.

"My favorite him is Billy Smith," she answered, "but I don't think he even likes me!"

* * *

The teacher was trying to explain ethical behavior to her class.

"One summer," she told them, "I worked in a gift shop. A woman came in and made a rather large purchase. In fact, it came to almost one hundred dollars. The woman paid with a one-hundred-dollar bill. I gave her the change and her purchase, and she left.

"I was standing there, fingering the bill, when all at once, it separated in my hands. The woman had really given me two one-hundred-dollar bills that were stuck together. The woman didn't know she had done this, and there was no one else in the store but me.

"Now, can anyone tell me what ethical problem I faced at that point?"

One young man raised his hand and was recognized.

"Sure," he said, "do you or do you not share it with the boss?"

SPECIAL NOTE: *Morality, religion, and God are always touchy subjects, since such a wide variety of beliefs is represented in your classroom and, most likely, in your audience. Children, who lack adult sensitivity, often treat these subjects in a more open, outspoken manner. An anecdote that relates a humorous classroom incident involving children's honesty in these areas will usually be well received by your audience.*

84

TOPICS:
Class activities; school assignments; teacher-student interaction

AUDIENCE:
Suitable for all adult audiences

"Johnny," said the teacher, "if you pull Mary Ellen's pigtail one more time, I'm going to keep you after school!"

Not five minutes later, Mary Ellen let out a shriek as Johnny pulled her hair. Johnny was assigned detention for that afternoon.

When the end of the school day came, Johnny began to leave with the rest of his first grade class, but he was stopped at the door by his teacher.

"Johnny," said the teacher, "I told you that you would have detention if you pulled Mary Ellen's hair. You did, and now you must stay after school."

"Wow!" said the young boy. "The kids told me that school isn't like home. They were right! When you guys say 'No'—you mean it!"

* * *

The teacher had taken her class of fifth-graders to an exhibit of modern art at a local museum. One of the exhibits was a huge painting by Jackson Pollock, the modern artist who painted by dripping paint on the canvas, throwing it, and even smearing it in places.

Two of the fifth-graders stood before the massive canvas and studied the explosion of squiggly lines and raw color. Finally, one of them turned to the other.

"If I had done something like that," the student complained, "they'd have made me clean up the art room and stay after school for a week!"

* * *

"Our teacher is a real cheapskate," said Jack one evening.

"What makes you say that?" asked his father.

"Well, Dad," the boy explained, "how much would you say a thimbleful of ink costs?"

"Certainly no more than a few cents," answered his father.

"You see!" the boy exclaimed. "And here she is getting all excited just because I spilled it on her new dress!"

*   *   *

When the teacher came in early from recess to set up for her new class, she found one of the boys under her charge seated at a desk, studiously writing out a math assignment.

"Well," she said, "I'm certainly glad to see you applying yourself to your studies. Tell me, Jeffrey, how long have you been working here?"

The boy replied honestly, "Ever since you came in the door, ma'am."

*   *   *

"Tommy," said the teacher, "I've never seen you do such terrible homework. Why, every answer is wrong. How do you account for that?"

"Ma'am," said Tommy, "when you were little, did your father ever insist on helping you with your homework?"

*   *   *

As part of a class counseling project, the teacher made "appointments" with each of her students during the regularly scheduled recess period. At each session, the teacher would talk openly with the student about his or her concerns, class work, problems, and so on.

On one particularly beautiful spring day, little Tommy was scheduled for an "appointment," and he dutifully showed up at the teacher's desk even as his eyes followed his classmates out to the playing field.

"Well, Tommy," said the teacher, "what would you like to talk to me about?"

"Ma'am," said Tommy, "if it's all the same to you, about two minutes would be just fine!"

*   *   *

"Just think," the teacher told the class, "some of the greatest discoveries have taken place in odd situations.

"For example, Archimedes discovered the principles of buoyancy while taking a bath, and Sir Isaac Newton discovered gravity while sitting under a tree.

"Now, children," she concluded, "what lesson can we gain from this?"

One hand was raised, and the teacher called upon the little boy.

"It shows us," said the student, "that if we spend all our time in school studying out of books, we ain't likely to learn a darn thing!"

SPECIAL NOTE: *While these stories are short, do not underestimate the value of their humor. They all revolve around school assignments and schoolwork, and they can enliven any presentation to parents or educators.*

Afterthoughts

Perhaps the relationship between students and their teachers is at the heart of a successful education. That may be a broad statement to make, but if you consider the number of people in responsible positions who have credited their interest and success in their profession to the inspiration and guidance of a teacher, then perhaps the statement becomes very relevant indeed.

In this chapter, we have dealt with the lighter side of that relationship. We realize, of course, it is a relationship that can be fraught with conflict and turmoil. The end result, however, is of vital importance in the life of the child, and in the life of the teacher as well. Quite often, a moment of shared laughter, when teacher and student find a common ground for understanding, can be the start of that beneficial and fruitful relationship—or one more brick added to its foundation, making it stronger still.

It is laughter which will last a lifetime, and THAT is no small thing!

Part 7
It's the Little Things That Count

As the math teacher said after a day of teaching basic arithmetic to first-graders, "It's the little things that count!" Indeed, were it not for children, there would be no teachers. Each and every year, a new group arrives at every school, most of them filled with the wonder of it all, with minds like so many suitcases ready to be packed with essentials they will use again and again on their journey through life. It is quite true that the child begets the man, and it is with this child that we, as educators, are vitally concerned.

It is our contention that the most vital part of every child's education occurs in grades one through eight—what is commonly referred to as "elementary" school. There is nothing "elementary" about it, however, for each child is a complex oganism requiring the insight, expertise, and experience of each of his teachers to reach his full potential. It is during this time that the child will learn those basics which are the stepping stones to everything else he will learn and the foundation of a happy and productive life in society.

In this section, we will take a look at life in the elementary school as seen through the eyes of teachers, parents, and the children themselves. We will investigate the relationships between these three elements that make for moments of laughter—moments that are laughable when they occur and that are remembered throughout life.

85

TOPICS:
Pets; caring; love; death; a child's perception

AUDIENCE:
Suitable for all audiences

The first grade class kept a pet gerbil in the room. Everyday, one of the students would feed it, clean its cage, and care for it. One morning, however, the class arrived to find their pet apparently lifeless in the bottom of the cage.

They were heartbroken. Tears flowed and chins quivered. Not a dry eye could be seen, and the teacher was having a difficult time calming them down. Finally, she hit upon an idea.

"Children," she said, "we will have a funeral for our dear pet gerbil."

She began organizing the affair.

For the coffin, she filled a cardboard box with tissue paper and had the children decorate it. Other children made a miniature headstone. Still others composed speeches telling how much the animal would be missed. Finally, they formed a procession with some carrying the casket while the others followed. Two boys dug a fine grave. As the teacher expected, their sorrow was soon eased by the activity of the gerbil's funeral.

The class filed out to the playground and stood in solemn rows as the bearers brought the sad burden and placed it in the tiny hole. Then the whole class sang one of their favorite songs. Finally, the teacher announced that following the burial, there would be milk and cookies for everyone. The entire class was smiling now from the sheer beauty of the event.

All at once, there was a small scraping sound inside the box. Slowly the cover moved and the gerbil poked his head out and looked around. The class stood with their mouths open in wonder.

For a long moment, no one spoke, then two boys came forward.

"Miss Jones," one of them whispered, "does this mean we don't get the milk and cookies?"

SPECIAL NOTE: *Since most elementary classrooms we know of have some sort of pet or terrarium, this story goes over well with elementary educators. On the serious side, it might also be used to lead into a discussion of what children should be told about death and dying.*

86

TOPICS:
Small children; misunderstanding; spelling

AUDIENCE:
Suitable for all audiences, particularly parents

The school secretary had to leave the office for a moment, so when the phone rang, there was no one to answer it except a first grade student who had been sent there with a message from his teacher. Consequently, he picked up the phone and said "Hello."

On the other end of the line was a parent who wanted to talk to the principal.

"There's nobody here but me," said the child.

"Well," said the parent, "could you take a message and give it to the principal?"

"Sure!" was his happy reply.

"All right, tell the principal that Mrs. Morton called, and she wants. . ."

"'Scuse me, ma'am," said the lad. "What's the name?"

"Morton," the woman said. "That's M-O-R-T-O-N—Morton."

There was a long pause on the line.

"Is something wrong?" asked the woman.

"Ma'am," said the boy, "do you know how to make an M?"

SPECIAL NOTE: Even the easiest of tasks which we adults take for granted is a major chore to a young child. This is a good reminder that the basics, as they are called, do not come naturally but are the result of proper training and hard work.

87

TOPICS:
Rural life; responsibility; taking the blame

AUDIENCE:
Suitable for all audiences

The teacher in a rural school district was driving along a country road one late afternoon when she saw one of the boys from her eighth grade class standing beside an overturned hay wagon, the hay piled high on the road.

"Jimmy," she asked, "what happened?"

"Hello, Mrs. Smith," said the lad. "I wasn't looking where I was driving the team, and the whole wagonload of hay just fell over. I unhitched the team, and they'll get home by themselves, but now I got this responsibility to . . ."

"Jimmy," interrupted the teacher, "I think it's wonderful and very mature of you to accept responsibility like that, and you should be rewarded. I want you to come with me, and I'm going to give you a piece of the pie I just baked."

"Well, gee thanks, ma'am, but, you see, I got the responsibility to . . ."

"I know," the teacher interrupted again, "but the hay will still be there when you get back. I insist."

With a shrug of his shoulders, Jimmy drove home with the teacher and had two helpings of apple pie and three glasses of milk.

"There, now," said the teacher when Jimmy had put down his napkin. "That's better isn't it?"

"That was sure good, ma'am," said Jimmy, "but do you think you could drive me back now. You see, I got the responsibility to . . ."

"Certainly," said the teacher, "and I have to say again how I admire the way you take responsibility for your actions. Don't you think, however, that it might be a better idea if I drove you to your house, and we got your father to help you clean up that hay?"

"That's just it, ma'am," Jimmy said as he stretched listlessly. "My pa was sitting on the hay when it turned over, and for all I know, he's still under that pile on the road. So I figure I got the responsibility to dig him out before nightfall!"

SPECIAL NOTE: *You could use this story for many reasons. It can lead into a discussion of responsibility, behavior standards, the value of listening, the wonderful interplay of cultures, and so forth. It is also just plain funny.*

88

TOPICS:
Field trip; bad news; manners; a child's perspective

AUDIENCE:
Suitable for all audiences, particularly educators

The school had gone on a picnic in a local nature preserve, and the teacher was enjoying some temporary peace and quiet because the principal had volunteered to take her class on a nature hike.

She was resting comfortably under a tree when she noticed one of her second-graders walking slowly toward her, eating what looked to be a peanut butter and jelly sandwich.

Slowly the child approached until he stood directly before the teacher.

"Miff Josnes," he muttered through a mouth full of sandwich, "mffgh weerg nuffle blidph."

"Billy," said the teacher, "I can't understand a word you say. And, haven't I told you that it's impolite to talk with your mouth full? Now, sit down over there and finish your sandwich; then come and tell me clearly what you want to say."

The boy nodded, took a seat beneath an adjacent tree, and took fifteen minutes to polish off the sandwich. Finally, he smacked his lips and walked over to the teacher.

"Well, Billy," said the teacher, "now that you've finished your sandwich and no longer have your mouth full, what did you want to tell me?"

"Only that the principal needs your help," said Billy. "She fell in the lake, and I think she's drowning."

SPECIAL NOTE: This story always gets a howl from an audience of teachers; even more so if the principal of their school is very popular. It's a good story for faculty get-togethers and dinners.

89

TOPICS:
Report cards; grades and grading; poor marks

AUDIENCE:
Suitable for parents and educators

Little Tommy entered the room and stood before his father. Slowly, he handed his father a folded sheet of paper.

"Dad," he said, "here's my report card."

"Thank you, Son," said his father, "but what's that other paper you have there?"

"Grandma gave it to me," the child said sweetly. "It's your report card from the fourth grade. I just wanted it handy in case you started screaming!"

*   *   *

One bright and cold January day, Mary came in from school with her report card. Naturally, her mother was anxious to see it.

"Before I show you this card," said the child, "may I ask you a question?"

"Why, certainly," said Mother.

"Okay," continued Mary. "What holiday did we celebrate just a few weeks ago?"

"Why, Christmas, of course," said her mother, "but what does that have to do with your report card?"

"I just want you to remember that all across America, things are always marked down after the holiday!"

*   *   *

Billy was getting poor grades in school, and both his parents and the teacher had been working very hard to improve the situation. One day, he came running in from school, shouting as loud as he could.

"Ma! Ma!" he exclaimed, "I got 100 in school today!"

"Billy!" rejoiced his mother. "That's wonderful. I'm going to make a special dinner, and we can surprise your daddy!"

Mother outdid herself preparing an outstanding meal. When it was finished, she announced to the father that they were celebrating because their son had gotten 100 in school.

"Tremendous!" the father shouted, barely able to contain his joy." Tell me about it. What subject was it in?"

"It was in *two* subjects," boasted Billy. "I got a 52 in history and a 48 in math!"

* * *

Little Sally slammed the report card down on the table before her mother and father.

"I would just like you to remember," she said, "that there was a whole lot less to learn when you were my age!"

* * *

"What material," asked the teacher, "gives off the most heat?"

"Paper, ma'am," answered the child.

"Why do you say that?" the teacher inquired.

"Well, every time I show my father my report card," the child answered, "you should see how red and sweaty he gets!"

* * *

The teenager marched into the living room and placed the report card, face down, before his mother and father.

"Before you turn that over," said the boy, "I want you to pause and consider that at least half of all social scientists believe heredity is the deciding factor in a child's development!"

SPECIAL NOTE: While poor grades in school are definitely nothing to laugh at, we all remember our own anxiety each time report cards were distributed. Perhaps it is this memory that makes stories about report cards such favorites with parents and educators alike.

90

TOPICS:
Oneupmanship; boasting and bragging; misinformation

AUDIENCE:
Suitable for all audiences, particularly parents

Normally, the class got along quite well. There was bound to be trouble, however, whenever two small members of the class got together. One was the daughter of a minister, a local "pillar of the community," while the other was the daughter of the town's mayor, a highly political person who maintained a very visible public image. The two girls fought almost constantly.

One day, they were in the middle of a shouting match.

"My father's more important than your father!" they screamed simultaneously.

"Oh, yeah?" said the daughter of the minister. "Well, last month my father bought a chicken, and that chicken lays an egg every day!"

"That's nothing!" shouted the daughter of the mayor. "Last night I heard my father talking on the telephone, and he said that the way things are going it looks like he's going to lay a cornerstone every week!"

SPECIAL NOTE: Children are often fiercely proud of their parents, as any elementary school educator will tell you, so this story has the ring of truth. It also conveys the fact that children very often misinterpret what they hear their parents say. For all these reasons, this story is especially appreciated by an audience of parents.

91

TOPICS:
First aid; health; emergencies; misinterpretation

AUDIENCE:
Suitable for all audiences

The class had just completed a unit on health with concentration on first aid. As part of the first-aid instruction, the teacher emphasized stopping the flow of blood by pressure or, in severe cases, by the use of a tourniquet. When a tourniquet is applied, explained the teacher, it is generally tied between the wound and the heart. The class then pointed out places where the tourniquet would be applied for major wounds on legs and arms.

The teacher was satisfied that the children had a firm grasp of first aid. The follow-up test showed that they had learned the material well, including the placement of a tourniquet.

The day after the test, it chanced that one little girl stood on a chair to get a book from a high shelf. The chair went out from under her, and she fell several feet, grazing her forehead and causing a small gash on her chin.

You guessed it. The teacher arrived just in time to stop the little boy who, with a smile of benign charity on his face, was rapidly tightening the belt he had slipped around the little girl's neck!

SPECIAL NOTE: *The moral of this story is something every teacher knows. Just because a student can give the right answer does not mean that the student has LEARNED the material or thoroughly understands it. Because imparting that understanding is the goal of every educator, this story serves as an excellent lead-in to a motivational speech for teachers, such as at the start of a new school year or the launch of a school-wide project.*

92

TOPICS:
Siblings; calling the home; a child's view

AUDIENCE:
Suitable for all audiences, particularly parents and educators

Johnny was not doing too well in his first-grade studies, and the teacher debated calling home and informing Johnny's mother. The teacher did not want to alarm the woman needlessly, but she felt that a push from home might get Johnny set on the right track.

Therefore, one afternoon when the children had gone home for the day, the teacher called Johnny's home. It was Johnny, himself, who answered the phone.

"Johnny," said the teacher, "this is Miss Wilson from school. Please let me speak with your mother."

"Gosh, Miss Wilson," came the voice from the other end of the line, "I can't do that. My mother's not here."

There was a perceptible pause, and then Johnny added, "But, I can let you talk to my sister, if that's okay?"

Miss Wilson thought for a moment. Many times an older sibling can be a great help with a younger brother or sister. Sometimes the younger child will take an older brother or sister's advice before that of parents or teachers. Therefore, Miss Wilson said, "All right, Johnny, please put your sister on the phone."

There was a clunk as Johnny set down the receiver followed by an interminable wait which stretched from a minute to five to ten. Miss Wilson was becoming agitated with the waiting.

Finally, there was a sound at the other end, and Johnny was back on, obviously out of breath.

"Miss Wilson," the boy panted, "I'll have my sister to the phone in a minute."

"Johnny, wait!" said the teacher. "If your sister is busy now, she can call me back when she's free."

"Oh, no, Miss Wilson," said Johnny, "it's okay. She'll be here in a minute. It's just that I'm having a lot of trouble lifting her out of her crib!"

SPECIAL NOTE: *Perhaps the moral of this story is that educators should never assume anything. However, it is true that older siblings have an effect upon younger ones and this could be the beginning of a meaningful discussion on that topic.*

93

TOPICS:
Wrong answers; quick thinking

AUDIENCE:
Suitable for both parents and educators

Said the teacher to her fifth grade class, "Who is responsible for the burning of Atlanta?"

"Honest, teacher, it wasn't me!" said one youngster.

"He's tellin' the truth," added another. "I was with him all morning, and he didn't do nothin'!"

* * *

"Billy," said the teacher, "if the emperor of Russia was called the czar, what were his children called?"

"I know," said Billy with a smile, "they were called czardines!"

* * *

"If the plural of *man* is *men*, and the plural of *woman* is *women*," asked the teacher, "then who can tell me the plural of *child?*"

The lad so questioned thought for a moment, looked at the teacher with a puzzled expression, and said, *"Twins?"*

* * *

"All right, Bobby," asked the teacher, "what is a synonym?"

"A synonym," answered Bobby, "is a word you use on compositions that means the same thing as the first word you wanted to use but couldn't spell!"

* * *

The teacher was trying to convey to her class the value of politeness.

"Let's suppose," she said, "that you were at the dinner table and you said, 'Excuse me, would you please pass the butter,' and later you said, 'That was a delicious meal,' and after that you said, 'Thank you for the dessert; it was quite good.' What would you be doing?"

"Easy," said one lad. "I'd be having dinner at somebody else's house!"

*   *   *

"Suppose there were four elephants in a row," said the teacher. "One of these elephants turns around and says, 'I see three trunks.' Now, which elephant would that be?"

"None of them," shouted one youngster.

"Billy," said the teacher, "please think again. They are in a row, and one of them says, 'I see three trunks.'"

"Miss Jones," insisted Billy, "the answer is none of them. You know darn well that elephants can't talk!"

*   *   *

"Mary," said the teacher, "please complete this: I will not go; you will not go; he will not go; we will not go. . ."

"Golly, Miss Jones," continued Mary, "there's not gonna be nobody there!"

*   *   *

"And what," inquired the teacher, "is the best way to take cod liver oil?"

Answered one youngster, "With a fork!"

SPECIAL NOTE: *Both parents and teachers seem to delight in these clever answers given by children to teacher's questions. They can be put into any address to make it lively and establish audience rapport.*

94

TOPIC:
Logic; fighting; children's squabbles; using your mind

AUDIENCE:
Very good with parents and educators

"So many of this world's troubles could be solved," said the teacher, "if we only used reason and logic. When two people have a disagreement, for example, they should sit down together and try to reason it out. They should use logic and calmly try to determine a satisfactory method for settling their disagreement."

The class seemed to agree, and the teacher felt very good about imparting this moral message to her charges. The feeling did not last too long, however, because that very day two boys from her class were sent to her for fighting on the playground during recess.

"I'm disappointed," she told them. "Just this morning, didn't we have a long talk on settling our differences in a reasonable and logical manner?"

"Sure, Miss Smith," said one boy who sported a magnificent black eye. "That's just what we were doing."

"What?" said the teacher. "How can that be?"

"Well," answered the lad, "you said we should use reason and logic and try to calmly find a way to settle our argument, right?"

"Yes, I did, but. . ."

"So," the boy continued, "when Peter said he could beat me up, and I said I could beat him up, we calmly sat down and logically decided that the only way to see who was right was to have a fight!"

SPECIAL NOTE: This story goes over well with both parents and educators, as most of them accept the sad, but true, fact of school life: children fight! Usually, however, differences are forgotten after such an altercation, and the combatants become fast friends. In your talk, it would be good to emphasize that, although we do not condone such behavior, we must understand that children often do not see things the way we do.

95

TOPICS:
Pretending; children at play; a child's imagination

AUDIENCE:
Suitable for all audiences

The kindergarten teacher was urging the children to use their imaginations.

"You must really pretend when you play," she told them. "You have to use your imagination so you will *feel* what it is like to be a tree or a cat or a chair."

With this, she organized the children into play groups, and she traveled from gathering to gathering, commenting on the marvelous things the children had come up with using their imaginations.

The teacher's smile faded quickly, however, when she came up to one group. Little Annie was lying on a table, and the bright, new yellow dress she had worn that morning had been ruined. Large holes had been snipped away by scissors or ripped by many hands.

"Children!" exclaimed the teacher. "Whatever are you doing?"

"We're playing delicatessen," answered little Annie from the table.

"Delicatessen?" murmured the teacher.

"Yep," said one lad who was obviously the shopkeeper, "and Annie's the Swiss cheese!"

SPECIAL NOTE: We can't advise our children to do something and then become angry with them when they follow our advice. Parents seem particularly appreciative of this story, perhaps because they have had very similar experiences.

96

TOPICS:
Grief; emotions; a child's view of death

AUDIENCE:
Especially suitable for parents and educators

"For tonight's assignment, class," said the teacher, "I want you to write a composition of fifty words on the topic 'Why I Love My Pet.'"

With that, one little girl in the first row began to shake and then to openly sob and wail. It was dismissal time, so the teacher let the rest of the class go and went to comfort the child.

"Mary Lou," said the teacher, "what's the matter?"

"You want us to write about our pet," sniffed Mary Lou, "and that reminded me that my kitty died!"

"I'm sorry, sweetheart," soothed the teacher. "When did your kitty pass on?"

"About a year ago," answered the child.

"A year?" said the teacher. "Isn't that a long time to be grieving for your cat? Why, my favorite aunt died a year ago, and I don't cry anymore."

"Sure," sobbed Mary Lou, "but I'll bet you didn't take your aunt and raise her from a kitten!"

SPECIAL NOTE: Your audience will respond favorably to this tender story. Most parents and educators have witnessed the strong attachments that children are capable of forming. The important point to make is that children's emotions aer very fragile and require special handling. This is especially good as a lead-in to a discussion of how to handle death and dying with children.

97

TOPICS:
Nature; outdoor life; acting without thinking

AUDIENCE:
Suitable for all audiences

The urban elementary class had taken a field trip to a local farm, and the teacher was explaining to them the wonders of nature.

They walked past fields of growing corn and wheat and barley and came at last to a section of land where the teacher had a special surprise for them.

"And this, children," she said, "is where they grow blackberries. These are the bushes. Now, I have a special treat for you. Farmer Smith has told me that you may pick and eat as many of these berries as you wish. Who wants to eat the first berry?"

Contrary to what she expected, there were no volunteers. Then, one boy asked tentatively, "How are we to do that, Miss Jones? There are no plates or forks or anything."

"Tommy," smiled the teacher, "we are outdoors now, and no one will mind if we use our hands. Just reach down, grab a berry, and pop it in your mouth. Here, watch me."

And Miss Jones reached down, grabbed a berry, and popped it in her mouth. She took one swallow and addressed the class.

"Now," she said, "are there any questions?"

"Just one," said the same lad. "How many feet does a blackberry have?"

"Tommy," laughed the teacher, "berries don't have any feet."

"Then I don't know how to tell you, Miss Jones," said the boy, "but you just ate a caterpillar!"

SPECIAL NOTE: Children and the outdoors often seem made for one another. Even so, some interesting and humorous things can happen when we set about instructing children in the use of their natural playground. This story will bring a smile to any adult, whether city or country dweller.

98

TOPICS:
Homework; helping children with assignments

AUDIENCE:
For all audiences, particularly parents

"Dad," said eight-year-old Louise, "you know those math problems you helped me with last night? Well, every one of them was wrong!"

"Good grief," said father, "what did the teacher say?"

"She didn't yell or anything," said Louise. "In fact, she said to tell you that your answers were closer than any other father's!"

SPECIAL NOTE: Helping with the homework is a practice that has been in good standing for centuries and is likely to remain so. This story might lead into a discussion on how to do so in a proper manner.

Afterthoughts

Children are a never-ending source of humor, just as they are an inexhaustible well of wonder and joy and sorrow and marvel. Hopefully, these stories of small children interacting with teachers and peers will bring a smile to everyone's lips and help us to appreciate and remember the wonder and confusion, the happiness and tears, the pleasures and the pains of that special time in everyone's life.

And, if we remember, perhaps we can rededicate ourselves to helping our own children through this often difficult time. Perhaps we can strive to work for each child to reach his or her full potential. Perhaps we can be there—when times are rough, to smooth the road—when times are good, to share the laughter. Certainly, every child will benefit from that.

And, it won't hurt the future of the world any, either.

Part **8**
Let's Keep It in the Family

M ost of us, we are certain, would agree that the family is the cornerstone of life in America. Yes, divorce rates may soar, and newspapers may be filled with stories of children torn apart by prolonged custody battles in courts, but the family still stands as the single, most enduring center of refuge, nourishment, and growth for the child in today's world.

There have been many studies of families to be sure, and most of them were conducted by people far wiser than we. Still, and for what it's worth, we have our own theory as to what the single characteristic of the loving, nurturing family is today and will remain in the future. Invariably, the families we have seen who produce loving and caring children are those in which there is a great deal of laughter along with the love.

Perhaps it is just our point of view, but the parents who can see their offspring throw up on the new sofa just when company arrives at the front door—and still laugh about it—have made that incident a moment of shared love rather than a point of contention between parent and child. The latter attitude leads to repressed hostilities and smoldering frustrations; the former is another gem added to the treasure chest of memories shared by a family. Children cannot help but sense this love, and it cannot help but have a beneficial effect on them.

Let's keep that in mind as we look at the funnier side of life in the family.

99

TOPICS:

Morality; embarrassment; shame; learning social mores

AUDIENCE:

Suitable for all audiences, particularly parents

When four-year-old Beth had tried to lie her way out of a who-knocked-over-the-lamp scenario, Mother had taken her aside and tried to explain to her the value of always telling the truth.

"Not only will you never have to worry that someone will find out that you were lying," said Mother, "but you will have a very good feeling inside from knowing that you did the right thing. When you tell the truth, you glow inside."

Beth listened and took this all in. Then, she confessed to having knocked over the lamp. Mother praised her honesty and gave her a cookie, and, indeed, Beth was radiant with the truth.

The next day, as Beth and Mother were driving downtown, Mother, in a weak moment, took her eyes off the road to look in a shop window, and had a close encounter with a mailbox on the corner. The mailbox was fine, but the car had a vivid, deep scratch down its entire right side.

That night, Beth walked into the living room just as Mother was explaining to Father what had happened.

"I just don't know," Mother was saying. "When I came out from shopping, there was our car in the middle of the parking lot with this huge scratch, and there was no one else around."

At which point, there was a power failure, and every light in the house went out.

"Oh, Mommie!" squealed Beth. "That was such a big fib, God took away all of the glow!"

SPECIAL NOTE: *Your audience will respond well to this touching story that also reminds us that children are literal creatures—they rarely see shades of meaning but are prone to accept only the literal content of our statements.*

100

TOPICS:
Music lessons; parental discipline; children and good behavior

AUDIENCE:
Suitable for all adult audiences

Two delivery men from a local department store were delivering a sofa to a house in town. When they had parked their truck they heard piano music coming from their destination. It was slow and labored, and the men surmised that it was a child practicing his or her lesson.

When they rang the doorbell, the music stopped, and the door was opened by a child of about seven. The boy was dressed in freshly pressed trousers, a snow-white shirt, a blazer and a tie, and his shoes were shined to a mirror finish.

The men could not help but stare at a child so neatly dressed who so assiduously practiced the piano on a lovely spring day when most boys would be out playing ball or just getting dirty.

"Son," one of them finally said, "we have a delivery for your mother. Is she at home?"

The little boy stared past the men at the bright sunshine, then at the piano where he had been practicing, and finally at his immaculate clothing.

"Come on," said the lad, "what do you think?"

SPECIAL NOTE: *Of course, if left to their natural desires, most children would rather play than practice a piano, or even go to school for that matter. Use this story as a gentle reminder to your audience that kids need time to just be kids and to enjoy the freedom of childhood.*

101

TOPICS:
Religion; brothers and sisters; teenagers

AUDIENCE:
Suitable for all adult audiences

It wasn't easy raising a family on a minister's salary, but they had always managed somehow until recently. The couple's teenage daughter had begun to ask for more and more—a stereo; new dresses; her own phone; a TV for her room. The list seemed endless, and there was simply no money for it in the budget.

Therefore, the minister thought it was time to have a talk with his daughter. They talked for over an hour, but he couldn't make her see that the items she wanted were out of reach.

Finally, in frustration, the minister shouted, "Don't you realize that your possessions merely drag you down to hell?"

"What?" said his daughter, and her whole demeanor changed.

Sensing that he had hit the mark, the minister continued, talking about being owned by one's possessions and an over-concern with worldliness. He ended with the statement that had been successful: "So you see, it's our possessions that drag us to hell."

"Daddy," she said, "I never realized. I don't want any of those new things I asked for. And I'm even going to start giving away some of the possessions I have now."

"Good girl," said her father. "Whom will you give them to?"

"Do possessions really drag us down to hell?" she asked.

"They certainly do," affirmed her father.

"In that case," she said with a bright smile, "I'll give them all to my little brother!"

SPECIAL NOTE: *Is there a parent anywhere who has not witnessed sibling rivalry within his or her own family? That seems to be as natural a part of growing up as playing. In most cases, it is nothing to worry about and may even be a source of family humor. This story gets an understanding laugh from any audience!*

102

TOPICS:
High society; manners; embarrassing moments; children and adults

AUDIENCE:
Suitable for all adult audiences, particularly parents

Mother was going to hold a very fashionable party in her home with a very impressive guest list that included the president of her husband's company, the mayor, and local political dignitaries. Consequently, she had rehearsed and rehearsed her six-year-old daughter and her four-year-old son on exactly how they must behave at the gathering.

"If you want me for anything," the mother told them, "don't pull on my dress. Just say in a loud, clear voice, 'Excuse me, Mother,' and then state what you have to say. Also, there will be many people at the party that you don't know, so when you talk about someone, you say, 'The gentleman would like. . .' or 'The lady prefers. . .' Do you understand?"

Both children affirmed that they did, indeed, understand. Mother even held a rehearsal for them. They performed like troupers.

The night of the party arrived, and all seemed to be going very well. The guests were enjoying themselves, and the children were the perfect, well-mannered hosts one reads about in books on etiquette.

Suddenly, Mother felt a sharp tug at her dress, and there was her daughter motioning for Mother to bend down.

"Mommie," the girl whispered, "I want to tell you something."

"Darling," her mother said through the clenched teeth of a forced smile, "I thought I told you not to tug on Mommie's dress this evening!"

"But, Mommie," the child continued to whisper, "I have to tell you that. . ."

"Darling," said her mother a bit firmer this time, "if you wish to tell me something, you know how to go about it and what to say. Do it the way I told you."

Mother smiled at the guests who surrounded her. They, in turn, smiled and gave knowing nods as if to affirm the difficulty of raising a child.

The little girl looked at the guests, then at her younger brother across the room, and finally at her mother.

"All right," she said with a shrug.

Clearing her throat, and in a loud, deep voice, she said, "Excuse me, Mother, but I should like to tell you that the very young gentleman on the other side of the room has just lost his pet frog in the avocado dip!"

SPECIAL NOTE: *Children can sometimes say the most embarrassing things at exactly the time you want them to be quiet. This story is very effective if you tell it as if you were the parent involved. Do it that way, and it's guaranteed to break the ice with any audience.*

103

TOPICS:
Manners; a situation backfires; children and manners

AUDIENCE:
Suitable for all audiences, particularly parents

Seven-year-old Maryann had been sent an invitation to attend a birthday party for the son of her father's boss. Naturally, both her father and mother insisted she go.

On the day of the party, Mother took Maryann aside and coached her on how she should behave at the birthday party.

"Remember," said her mother, "that little boy is the son of Daddy's boss, so I want you to be extra nice and extra polite. If his mother talks to you, I want you to be certain to be nice, and let her know who you are."

"If she talks to me, Mommie," said the little girl, "what should I say?"

"Just be honest," her mother advised, "but don't just say 'Yes' or 'No.' Make polite conversation. You've been around when Daddy and I have guests over, and you've heard how we talk politely about all sorts of things. Try to talk to her that way."

The time came and little Maryann was off to the party. All through the afternoon, Maryann's mother was hoping her daughter would make a favorable impression on the boss's wife, and, when Maryann walked through the door several hours later, her mother was upon her at once, asking her all about the party.

"It was neat," said Maryann. "They even had a magician and a clown!"

"That's lovely, dear, but what about the lady. Did the lady speak to you?"

"Oh, yes, she did."

"And?" the mother asked. "What did you say?"

"Well," said Maryann, "she asked me my name and I told her, just like you said."

"Good, good."

"And, then she asked me what I thought of the party."

"Yes, and what did you say?"

"I was going to say 'It's neat,'" said Maryann, "but I remembered what you said about making polite conversation and talking like you and Daddy do at parties."

Mother beamed with pride.

"So I told her, 'With all the money that old skinflint saves on my daddy's salary, you'd think he could afford a bigger cake!' "

SPECIAL NOTE: Everybody likes stories where a plan of some kind backfires with humorous or embarrassing effect. This type of story carries the ring of truth. Many parents may vicariously experience the emotions undoubtedly felt by the mother at the end of this tale.

104

TOPICS:
Cultural events; music; misunderstanding; a child's
view

AUDIENCE:
Suitable for all audiences

Father decided that his son needed to be exposed to culture and refinement, so he bought three tickets to a local performance of an opera.

Before they left for the event, the father carefully explained the story of the work to his son, and he had even purchased an English translation of the libretto, which he went over word by word.

At the theater, the boy sat through the first act with a growing smile on his face. When it came time for intermission, the father was anxious to find out his son's reaction.

"It's great!" exclaimed the boy. "I really like the way that guy in the hole keeps stabbing the lady with the stick!"

"Just a minute," said the father. "the man to whom you refer is the conductor. He is standing in the orchestra pit. And, that stick is his baton. What's more, he is definitely *not* stabbing the lady."

"He's not stabbing her with the stick?"

"Of course not," fumed the father.

"Oh, yeah," demanded the boy. "Then how come every time he waves it at the fat lady, she runs around the stage and screams?"

*SPECIAL NOTE: Opera, like most cultural activities, is an acquired taste.
Use this story to make the point that while it is certainly
a good idea to expose children to all sorts of experiences,
we run into trouble when we expect them to see things
with adult eyes.*

105

TOPICS:
Honesty; moral values; money; shades of meaning

AUDIENCE:
Suitable for all audiences

Tommy came running into the house completely breathless and sank to the floor in exhaustion.

"Tommy," said his mother, "what's the matter?"

"Ma," panted Tommy, "I-I ran all the way. Look! Look at this!"

Tommy held out his hand, and in it was clutched a one-hundred-dollar bill.

"Tommy!" exclaimed his mother, "wherever did you get that money?"

"I was walking along Main Street," said the boy, "and I looked down on the pavement and there it was!"

"Tommy," said his mother, "you didn't take this money, did you?"

"No, Ma! It was lost, and I found it!"

"Are you certain it was lost?" asked his mother.

"Honest, Ma," protested Tommy, "I know it was lost. It was! I stood and watched the guy search for it for almost an hour!"

SPECIAL NOTE: Developing a sense of moral values is an essential part of the learning process and of growing up. Stories such as this make a fine beginning for a discussion group tackling the problem of exactly how to go about instilling these values.

106

TOPICS:
Safety; lifesaving; brothers; responsibility

AUDIENCE:
Suitable for all audiences

One late summer afternoon, Mother was going about her normal household chores when the back door slammed shut and six-year-old Billy came running in. The child was wet, soaked from head to toe. He was crying and blubbering, and he sported a technicolor black eye.

"Billy!" shouted his mother. "What happened?"

Before the child could stop crying long enough to answer, the back door slammed again, and his eight-year-old brother, Jimmie, came stomping into the house, obviously angry and upset.

"Boy," said Jimmie addressing his brother, "that's the last time I ever do anything nice for you!"

"Jimmie! Billy!" insisted their mother, "stop it this minute! Now, I want an explanation! What has been going on here?"

"You know how we had this class in first aid in school last year?" asked Jimmie. "Well, today we were walking over by the lake, and Bill fell in."

"He fell in?" repeated the startled mother.

"Yeah," continued Jimmie, "and after he swam out, I tried to give him mouth-to-mouth resuscitation, but he kept getting up and running away, and I had to hit him twice before he'd let me finish!"

SPECIAL NOTE: You might want to point out that children are always anxious to try out new things that they have learned. So much so, in fact, that they may create the opportunity if none presents itself.

107

TOPICS:
Faith; practicality; country life; ingenuity

AUDIENCE:
Suitable for all audiences, particularly parents

"Pa," said the farm boy at supper one evening, "I think that tomorrow morning I'll take my rifle and go hunt some rabbits."

"Good idea, Son," said his father. "They've been getting to our crops lately. We can also sell the pelts."

With that, Mary, the boy's seven-year-old sister, started to cry.

"I don't want Joe to hurt the bunnies!" she sniffled.

Gently, her father tried to explain that rabbits can often destroy a crop, that their livelihood depended on what they raised, and that the rabbits just had to be controlled. The child, however, was having none of it. She continued to sulk and act weepy all evening.

The next morning dawned bright and clear, and little Mary came bouncing down the steps and skipping into the kitchen where mother was working.

"Well," said Mother, "aren't we bright and happy this morning. I guess you thought over what Daddy said last night about the rabbits?"

"Better than that," the child said. "Last night, I prayed to God to make my brother miss every rabbit he shot at!"

"Oh, honey," said mother, "that's so sweet. But . . . if your brother does come home with some rabbits, maybe God doesn't want him to miss when he shoots. Did you think of that?"

"I sure did," said Mary, "so after I prayed, I came downstairs and took Daddy's pliers and twisted the sights on his rifle!"

SPECIAL NOTE: *Faith and practicality are a hard combination to beat. This story might well lead into any request for funds or parental assistance and volunteers. We have the faith, now what we need is the money (or time, volunteers, et cetera).*

108

TOPICS:
Discipline; experience; bad behavior; dealing with children

AUDIENCE:
Suitable for all adult audiences

The restaurant was rather crowded when a family consisting of a mother, father, and their four-year-old son came in and were seated. At first, everything went well, but soon the four-year-old began to get restless. He fidgeted and threw his napkin to the floor. When his parents tried to calm him, he screamed and began pounding on the table with his fists. Finally, he began taking food from his plate and throwing it at other tables. He was the epitome of the brat, and eyes everywhere turned to look at the spoiled child and his harried parents.

Finally, a rather distinguished looking gentleman got up from a nearby table and walked over.

"Excuse me, folks," he said to the parents, "but when I was a young man, I raised three brothers. Later, I married and raised seven children of my own. I wonder if you'd like to visit with my wife at our table for a moment and let me have a quiet talk with your son?"

The parents asserted that they had "talked" to the boy many times and all to no avail, but they agreed to let the man have his chance. They left the man with their son.

From across the room, they could not hear what was being said, but they watched as the man smiled and extracted a magazine from his pocket. He placed the magazine on the table and began to leaf through it page by page, talking to the child all the time. Finally, he folded the magazine, placed it back in his pocket and left the table.

The rest of the meal went flawlessly. The little boy sat quietly at the table and was as polite and mannerly as anyone could have wished for. He was the complete antithesis of the lad who had entered the restaurant.

It happened that both the family with the child and the distinguished man and his wife were leaving the place at the same time, and they met in the foyer.

"Sir," said the father of the boy, "I really have to thank you for what you did, but what *did* you do? I've tried showing him pictures in a magazine before, but it never had an effect like this."

"I didn't show him pictures," said the older man. "I laid the magazine down and said, 'Look at all the pages in this magazine. See how heavy it is. Now, if you don't shut up and behave, I'm going to roll up this magazine and smack you on the backside with it so hard, you won't sit down for a week!'"

SPECIAL NOTE: There is a time for reason, psychology, and logic, and there is a time for a more practical and direct approach. Parents are particularly fond of this story, we have found.

109

TOPICS:
Tardiness; a child's imagination; a child and God

AUDIENCE:
Suitable for all adult audiences

When Tommy came in from school, his mother was waiting for him with a stern look on her face.

"Tommy," she said, "come here this instant. The teacher just called from school to tell me that you were half an hour late this morning. You left here in plenty of time, young man. Now, what happened to make you so late?"

Tommy dug his heels in the carpet and stared at the floor.

"Well," he said, "I was going to school, and I was almost there, when all of a sudden this big tiger came out from behind a tree, and I didn't want the tiger to eat me, so I had to wait until the tiger went away, and that's why I was half an hour late for school."

"Young man," said his mother, "that is the most ridiculous story I have ever heard. I spoke with your teacher, and she said that she saw you from the window. You were in the playground playing with a little cat.

"Now, young man, I want you to go straight up to your room and say a prayer and ask God to forgive you for telling a lie to your mother! March!"

Tommy marched to his room and was in there for quite some time. Finally, his mother climbed the stairs to look in on her son.

"Well, Tommy," she said, "have you asked God to forgive you for what you said?"

"Yes, ma'am," was the reply.

"And do you think God has answered your prayer?"

"Yes, he has, ma'am. I prayed, and God answered me."

"Oh," said the mother skeptically, "and what did God say?"

"He said, 'Hey, Tommy, that's okay. The first time I saw that cat, I thought it was a tiger, too!'"

SPECIAL NOTE: *Children have vivid imaginations, and quite often, the line between imagination and reality is very fragile. Use this inspirational story as a reminder to everyone who works with children that it should be their goal to help young imaginations strive for attainable goals without ever losing sight of their childhood dreams.*

110

TOPICS:
Embarrassment; honesty; saying what one means

AUDIENCE:
Suitable for all audiences, particularly parents

A neighbor had invited the Jones family for dinner one evening. Mrs. Jones was a bit suspicious, since the families rarely shared a meal together, but the invitation was accepted, and at the appointed time, they arrived at the neighbor's house.

The reason for the invitation quickly became apparent, however, when the neighbors led them into the dining room which had been completely redecorated with new furniture, drapes, wallpaper, and carpet.

Appropriate words of praise and delight were exchanged, and the group retired to the living room. The host left to get hors d'oeuvres, and the hostess left to answer a phone call, so the Jones family was temporarily left alone, giving Mrs. Jones the opportunity to have a few words with Mr. Jones. Billy Jones took it all in silently.

Finally, dinner was served in the new dining room, and all progressed normally until dessert. Young Billy was offered a second helping of a particularly rich cake, and he readily accepted.

"Are you sure you should have a second helping, Billy," said his mother. "I don't want you becoming ill."

"It's okay, Mom," said little Billy. "I heard what you told Dad, but honest, the carpet and drapes don't make *me* want to throw up!"

SPECIAL NOTE: Embarrassment at the hands of one's own children seems to be a recognized part of parenthood. Of course, if Mrs. Jones hadn't criticized her neighbor's taste in front of Billy, it would not have happened. This might be a starting point for a discussion following the story.

111

TOPICS:
A child's view; religion; misunderstanding; mother
and father

AUDIENCE:
Suitable for all audiences, particularly parents

It was the Sunday School class for seven-year-olds, and the
minister had just finished his lesson. He asked the class if there were
any questions.

"Yes, sir," said one lad. "Is hell a disease?"

Since the lesson he had just given was about Noah and the flood,
the minister was somewhat taken aback by the question. However,
he believed that any honest question deserved an honest answer,
and he tried to give one on the level that the child would understand.

"Son," the minister said, "I have read some authors who
described evil or badness as a disease, but I've never heard of hell
being referred to in that way. Usually, it's referred to as a place. Does
that answer your question?"

"I guess so," said the boy.

"Why did you ask that, Son?" asked the minister.

"I was just curious to see if it was like the flu," stated the boy,
"because this morning I heard Mom tell our neighbor that if Dad was
late for supper tonight he was really going to catch hell!"

SPECIAL NOTE: Literal interpretation of what adults say is a characteristic of childhood that has led to many a misunderstanding. It is well to remember this when speaking to children in order to make our communications clear and exact.

112

TOPICS:
Short subjects

AUDIENCE:
Suitable for all audiences, particularly parents

Father had brought the boss home for dinner. Everything was going well until mother brought in the main course which was a magnificently done roast of beef.

"Ain't we gonna have turkey?" asked their son.

"I guess not, Son," said the father's boss. "What made you think we were?"

"This morning before Daddy left for work," the child told the father's employer, "I heard him tell Mommie that he was bringing the old bird home for supper!"

* * *

The mother and father had taken their small daughter to a fancy restaurant for the first time, and she was awed by everything, particularly the waitresses.

That night, she appeared in the living room dressed in her nightclothes and with a pencil and pad in her hands.

"Well, folks," she said, "I'm going upstairs to say my prayers. Now, who wants what?"

* * *

"Do you know what this is?" the woman asked the little girl who was visiting her daughter.

"Oh, yes," said six-year-old Betty. "It's a scale. We have one at home."

"And do you know how to use it?"

"Sure," said Betty, "I see my mommie use it every morning. I'll show you."

With that, Betty hopped on the scale, looked at the dial, jumped off, stamped her foot, and roared, "Damn, damn, damn, damn, damn!"

* * *

The family was shopping at a mall that had all kinds of stores, and they decided to treat their little girl. They bought her new shoes and a new dress which the child wore out of the store. Mother was going to have her own hair done, so on a whim they had the hairdresser do up the child's hair as well.

When they got home, the child hurried to the full length mirror in her parent's room and stood there admiring the finished image.

"Mommie," she asked, "The Reverend says that God made everybody. Did God make you and Daddy?"

"Yes, dear," smiled Mother, "He certainly did."

"Wow!" exclaimed the little girl still gazing into the mirror. "Has he ever improved his workmanship!"

*   *   *

"Gosh," said the six-year-old who answered the door, "you don't look like a fish!"

"Thanks, kid," said the teenage boy who was standing on the porch, "but why did you say that?"

"Because," said the youngster, "I just heard my sister tell Mommy that she finally got you hooked!"

SPECIAL NOTE: *These short anecdotes can be used separately or sprinkled through a speech to add warmth and humor wherever needed. We have found that they are particular favorites of parents.*

Afterthoughts

Throughout this chapter, we have tried to give many warm and humorous insights into family life. These are some of our favorite stories, and we hope they will gain special favor with you as well.

When you are telling these stories, you may use them as they are, of course, but it adds an extra touch of warmth and good rapport if you can personalize them in some way. Make yourself the mother or father in the story, or tell the story as if recalling the days when you were a child. You might also make it your child, or throw in the name of a local street or shop or school. Doing this, particularly if it is a story concerning the embarrassment of a parent and that parent is you, makes the story a hundred times better received by an audience and gains tremendous rapport.

Try it, and you'll see how well it works.

Part 9
Well-Roasted

Whether it is at a retirement dinner, a testimonial, or any other function where there is a guest of honor, one sure method of adding a little levity to the occasion and setting the audience at ease is the process of "roasting" the "man (or woman)-of-the-hour." Invariably, these are happy occasions, and the featured guest fully understands and expects to be put on the spot.

There are, however, a few rules that should be followed. It is always wise to advise the guest of honor beforehand of your intention to have a little fun at his or her expense and ask permission to proceed. Next, always be certain to deliver the stories with a twinkle in your eye and in a tone of voice that assures everyone this is merely good-natured bandying and has no other intent behind it. Finally, make certain that the material you use is so far-fetched and incredible that no one could ever take it seriously.

We feel that the following material fits the bill on all counts. We have personally used it and heard it used effectively on any number of occasions. Invariably, it received a great amount of laughter and applause, and, most importantly, the guest of honor laughed the loudest of all.

113

TOPICS:
Dullness; failure in communication

AUDIENCE:
Adults, especially friends of the subject of the story

The other day, I happened to be walking outside with Dr. Smith *(use the name of the guest of honor)*, when we noticed Mr. Jones *(use the name of a local principal, school board president, et cetera)* coming down the street carrying a large bag.

We stopped Mr. Jones and asked him what was in the sack, and he told us that he had some cats in the bag and was on his way to the local ASPCA to give them away.

Dr. Smith immediately brightened and remarked that he had always wanted a pet cat.

"If I can guess how many cats you have in the bag," Dr. Smith asked, "will you give me one?"

"Doctor," said Mr. Jones, "if you can guess how many cats I have in this bag, I'll let you have both of them."

(Wait for laughter to subside.)

Dr. Smith guessed three!

SPECIAL NOTE: *There are two laughs built in here, so be certain to wait until the first round subsides before delivering the "kicker" of the second punch line.*

114

TOPICS:

Fair punishment; dullness; punishment befitting crime

AUDIENCE:

Adults, friends of the subject of the story, especially individuals who have had to work with or under the subject of the story

I had a very unusual dream the other night which I'd like to share with you. In that dream, I saw Mr. Jones, Mr. Richards, and Dr. Smith. *(Use the names of people in the audience or other speakers on the dais. Use the name of the guest of honor last. You'll see why shortly.)* They were driving together when all at once there was this horrible accident and all three of them were lost forever.

For awhile, there was nothing but darkness, but presently, all three awoke to find themselves together in the lobby of a hotel. As they looked around, they could not help but notice there was no one else in the room but themselves, not even a desk clerk.

They were speculating about their situation when, from out of nowhere, a public address system snapped on, and a voice announced, "Welcome to Hotel Forever, where you will spend eternity!"

This rather upset the three, but they had little chance to talk about it before the PA system came on again, and a voice intoned, "MR. JONES, report to Room 100!"

All three of them went down the hallway to Room 100, and Mr. Jones opened the door.

Inside was a room which was shabby beyond belief, with threadbare carpeting and peeling wallpaper. Along one wall was a faded and lumpy sofa, and seated on it was a woman in a dirty housecoat with her hair in curlers and carrying a rolling pin who immediately jumped to her feet and began to berate Mr. Jones, telling him that she was going to give him a piece of her mind and waving the rolling pin in a highly threatening manner.

With that, the PA system snapped on again, and the voice said, "MR. JONES, FOR THE SINS YOU HAVE COMMITTED IN LIFE, YOU ARE CONDEMNED TO SPEND ETERNITY IN THIS ROOM WITH THIS WOMAN!" And, with that, the door slammed shut on Mr. Jones.

This left Mr. Richards and Dr. Smith roaming the halls and feeling rather shaken. Presently, however, another message came through on the PA: "MR. RICHARDS, report to Room 200!"

When they arrived at Room 200, and Mr. Richards opened the door, they were even more shocked than before. If possible, this room was in even worse condition than the first one. Plaster was cracking from the ceiling, empty beer cans littered the floor, and along one wall, on a broken-down sofa with the springs popping out of it, sat a woman, obviously intoxicated, with dirty, stringy hair, running mascara, and smeared lipstick.

At that moment, the PA system came on, and the voice said, "MR. RICHARDS, FOR THE SINS YOU HAVE COMMITTED IN LIFE, YOU ARE CONDEMNED TO SPEND ETERNITY IN THIS ROOM WITH THIS WOMAN!" And the door slammed shut on Mr. Richards.

That left Dr. Smith to roam the halls alone and shaken. It was not too long, however, before the voice was on the PA again, this time demanding, "DR. SMITH, report to Room 300!"

Well, I can tell you, when Dr. Smith finally arrived at Room 300, he was a nervous wreck. As he reached for the doorknob, his hand was shaking visibly. With great fear and effort, he opened the door, took one deep breath, and stepped inside.

The room was gorgeous! There were velvet drapes on the windows, a thick pile carpet on the floor, beautiful, floral-print wallpaper, and art masterpieces hanging in gold frames. Along one wall was a luxurious gold lamé sofa with silk pillows.

Dr. Smith was gazing around in astonishment, when the voice came on again and said, "DR. SMITH, SIT DOWN ON THE SOFA!"

Dr. Smith sat on the sofa.

"ARE YOU COMFORTABLE?" asked the voice, and Dr. Smith nodded that he was.

"WATCH THE DOOR," commanded the voice.

Dr. Smith turned his attention to the door. Presently it opened slowly and in walked none other than Jane Fonda dressed in a satin, off-the-shoulder evening gown and looking ravishingly beautiful.

Dr. Smith stood with his mouth hanging open, when all at once, the PA system snapped on again, and the voice intoned, "JANE FONDA, FOR THE SINS YOU HAVE COMMITTED IN LIFE . . ."

SPECIAL NOTE: *You will not have to go any further than that. The room will literally explode with laughter, and you will undoubtedly get a very good round of applause. Be certain to be dramatic as you describe each room and the VOICE. If you "ham it up," so much the better.*

This story can easily be adapted to a woman as the main subject by substituting characterizations of unappealing men in the shabby rooms and a current male movie or TV idol for the punch line.

Honestly, this is one of the best roast stories we have ever used. Try it; it gets results.

115

TOPICS:

Married life; health; exercise; having achieved
longevity

AUDIENCE:

Adults, particularly good if the subject's spouse is
present, and they have been married for a number of
years

One of the outstanding features of our guest this evening is the
fact that he has been married for over forty-three years. That, combined with the fact that he is also well-known for his fantastic good
health and robustness, led me to ask him the secret of both his long
life and his long and obviously happy marriage.

Dr. Smith was very generous, and he told me that there was one
secret that accounted for both his health and his happy marriage. It
seems that when he and Mrs. Smith were first married, they made a
pact. They knew that all married couples inevitably have arguments.
Consequently, they decided that whenever they had an argument,
the one who was in the wrong would go outside and walk around
the block four or five times.

Dr. Smith claims that it is absolutely amazing what forty-three
years of exercise like that did for his health!

SPECIAL NOTE: *Be certain to use the name of your guest of honor and*
the correct number of years he or she has been married.
We have found that this story works just as well for a
woman as for a man without any changes.

116

TOPICS:
Man-of-few-words; quietness and reserve; dullness

AUDIENCE:
Adults, particularly suitable if the guest is known for terseness of speech, the traditional man-of-few-words

You know, ladies and gentlemen, last year at this time, the pressures and stress of his job were really getting to Dr. Smith. Mr. Jones *(use the name of the local board president)* heard this fact and invited Dr. Smith and Mr. Richards, the high school principal, to spend a month at an isolated mountain cabin that Mr. Jones maintained. He assured Dr. Smith that there would be nothing but peace and quiet.

Consequently, the three of them left civilization and set up in the cabin deep in the woods.

If it was peace and quiet they wanted, that was exactly what they got. There was literally nothing to do but sit in the sunlight and gaze at the forest and the mountains.

For one week, no one said a word. Then, on the last day of that first week, Mr. Richards said, "Lovely day!"

Another week went by, and Mr. Jones said, "Yes, it certainly is!"

A third week went by when Dr. Smith slammed down the book he was reading, rose to his feet and proclaimed, "There's no use in staying here if you two keep talking all the time. I'm going home!"

SPECIAL NOTE: *As we said above, this is a particularly good story to use on someone who is not noted for his words or long speeches. You might follow this up, however, with reference to the subject's deeds which speak much louder than words.*

117

TOPICS:
Boring speeches; sanity; tedious subjects

AUDIENCE:
Adults, particularly good if the guest is noted for his or her speeches

Dr. Smith has always been known for his ability to deliver speeches. Therefore, the superintendent of the local hospital for the mentally ill asked Dr. Smith if he would consider giving a speech to the patients. Dr. Smith thought about this for awhile and finally consented to do it.

When Dr. Smith arrived at the hospital, the superintendent told him that although the audience posed no threat, they were likely to interrupt from time to time. He advised Dr. Smith that the best course of action was just to ignore the interruption and keep right on speaking.

The speech began, and to Dr. Smith's delight, the patients were quite attentive and appreciative. About the middle of the speech, however, one patient in the audience rose to his feet and proclaimed, "Good Lord! This is insane drivel. I've got to get out of here!"

Quickly, two attendants were at the man's side, and they led him gently from the room. Heeding the superintendent's advice, Dr. Smith continued as if nothing has happened.

Following the speech, the superintendent thanked Dr. Smith and expressed concern that the interruption had bothered his concentration.

"Oh, no," said Dr. Smith, "I was prepared, thanks to you, and I kept right on."

"Good," said the superintendent. "I'm as happy for you as I am for the patient."

"But," inquired Dr. Smith, "why are you happy for the patient?"

"Lord, man," replied the superintendent, "didn't you hear what he said. That's the first time he's had a sane moment in the last fifteen years!"

SPECIAL NOTE: *This is particularly good if the subject of your roast is well-known as a speaker. Any personal touches you could add that would make the speaker in this story more identifiable with your subject would add to its effect.*

118

TOPICS:
Toughness; perseverance; danger; a tough individual

AUDIENCE:
Adults, suitable for all occasions

I don't know whether you are aware of it, but we almost had a tragedy on our hands a few weeks ago. Let me tell you about it.

A traveling circus was passing through our town and had an accident at the traffic light on Main Street. No one was injured, but one of the cages carrying the wild animals fell and broke open, and a very dangerous lion was able to escape.

Naturally, the police were called, and through following up on the reports they received, they began to narrow down the whereabouts of the beast. They finally located the area where the lion had gone, and surrounded it. It was the block the school administration building is on.

Dr. Smith was unaware of the commotion outside as he went about his daily tasks. One of the secretaries heard the noise, however, and when she went to investigate, she opened the door to the building and came face-to-face with the lion.

The snarling beast jumped directly past her and into the administration building. It ran down the hall, past Dr. Smith's secretary, put its weight against the door of Dr. Smith's office, and, when the door gave, it jumped right into the room.

Dr. Smith's secretary immediately called Mr. Jones, the assistant superintendent.

"Come quickly," she shouted, "a raging lion has just entered Dr. Smith's office!"

Mr. Jones thought for a moment and said, "A lion, huh? Well, I was never particularly fond of lions, so if that dumb cat doesn't know any better than to disturb Dr. Smith when he's working, I'm afraid the beast will just have to take the consequences. I can't help him!"

(This is the first punch line. Wait for the laughter to die down before continuing.)

The good news is that the lion will be out of the hospital next week!

SPECIAL NOTE: Of course you will use the names of your local people and a local street in place of the one in the story. Also, narrate the progress of the lion in relation to the layout of your subject's office.

119

TOPICS:

Three short roasts involving the character of the subject

AUDIENCE:

Suitable for all subjects

. . .and, of course, there is the fact that Dr. Smith is a self-made man. Dr. Smith, himself, will tell you that what he did, he did on his own; that his words were his own words; that what he has become he has become of his own making. Yes, he will tell you that he is, indeed, a self-made man.

And that fact, ladies and gentlemen, has relieved God of an awesome responsibility!

*　　*　　*

It is a little known fact, but Dr. Smith very nearly did not become our superintendent.

You see, when he was being considered for the post, there was some question as to whether Dr. Smith could handle the pressures of the job. He was called before the board, therefore, for a rather grueling examination which took several hours filled with many question and answers. Finally, Dr. Smith was utterly exhausted.

"Look," he told the board, "I have the best qualifications of any of the candidates, and I'm the best person for the job. As I see it, you have only two choices: you can hire me, or you can go to hell!"

The president of the board told me that it was a very tempting alternative!

*　　*　　*

Recently, Dr. Smith was invited to attend a panel discussion. On the panel, in addition to Dr. Smith, were two clergymen and an atheist.

Naturally, the discussion got around to the subject of eternity and life after death. The panel talked on and on about heaven and hell and eternal life, but Dr. Smith said nothing. Finally, the moderator addressed Dr. Smith directly.

"Dr. Smith," she said, "we haven't heard anything from you on the subject."

"I'd rather not," replied Dr. Smith.

"Come, come, Doctor," said the moderator, "surely you have an opinion about heaven and hell."

"Of course," was his reply, "but, you see, I have so many friends in both places, that I don't want to take the chance of offending anyone!"

SPECIAL NOTE: These are short pieces that can be fit into a much longer speech. They are effective and should bring a chuckle or two. Again, any personalization of these stories to especially fit your subject will enhance their value.

120

TOPICS:
Popularity; good deeds; having to live with others

AUDIENCE:
Adults, particularly good if the subject of the roast is
extremely well-liked

Everyone knows how much Dr. Smith likes to participate in the
activities of our local schools. Last June, the eighth grade was having
a picnic at Lake LaGrande, and they invited Dr. Smith to attend. This
he did gladly.

Everything went very well. The luncheon was great, the
companionship excellent, and the early summer weather made the
landscape exquisite. Following lunch Dr. Smith decided to take a
walk and commune with nature.

It isn't very well-known, but Dr. Smith cannot swim. He took a
chance, therefore, when he stepped out on to a promontory which
overhung the lake. The view was so magnificent, however, that he
simply could not resist.

Sure enough, a loose rock gave way, and Dr. Smith plummeted
down the embankment and into the lake. The water at that point was
particularly deep, and although the fall did not injure him, he was
in real trouble as he began to sink rapidly.

He was going down for the third time, when he felt a hand grasp
his shoulder. Then, his head was pulled above water, and he was on
his back being towed into shore.

When he had resumed breathing regularly and had regained his
composure, Dr. Smith looked at his rescuer and found that it was
none other than one of the eighth grade boys who was on the picnic
with the class.

"Son," said Dr. Smith, "you saved my life! I was gone for certain
if you hadn't come along. How can I repay you?"

"Please, don't mention it," replied the boy.

"No, really," Dr. Smith continued, "that was a heroic deed, and
I want to do something."

"Honest, Dr. Smith," said the lad, "don't mention it!"

"But, I insist. . ."

"Look, Dr. Smith," affirmed the boy, "I have to live with the rest of the class for the next four years. Do you know what that would be like if they found out I saved you? So please, just don't mention it!"

SPECIAL NOTE: *We must give you some special insight about this story. Please do NOT use it if the subject is the least bit unpopular. In that case, the humor could be mistaken for vindictiveness or spite, and it would cast a shadow not only on the festivities but on you as well. If the subject is a well-liked, popular person, however, then there can be no doubt that it is all in fun, and everyone will enjoy it and laugh together.*

121

TOPICS:
Quick roasts for specific types of subjects

AUDIENCE:
Suitable for all adult audiences and subjects

IF THE SUBJECT IS PARTICULARLY THIN:

We have much for which to thank Dr. Smith. Not the least of which is the fact that we got in here this evening. You see, the manager had left his keys at home, but Dr. Smith was able to squeeze under the door and let us in!

* * *

IF THE SUBJECT IS PARTICULARLY HEAVY:

Yes, I have known Dr. Smith for a great many years. In fact, we go back so far, that I'm one of the few people who remember him when he was a mere shadow of his present self!

* * *

IF THE SUBJECT IS KNOWN FOR TALKING A GREAT DEAL:

I'll say this: Dr. Smith is certainly well-known. Just a few weeks ago, I visited a high school class in anthropology. The teacher asked if I would like to test the class, so I picked on one very bright-looking young man.

"Son," I asked, "where is the Tower of Babel located?"

Without a second's hesitation, the boy replied, "That's easy! It's at the school administration building!"

(Use the address of the subject's place of work, such as the administration building if it's a superintendent or the school if it's a principal, et cetera.)

* * *

IF THE SUBJECT HAS A DOCTORATE:

You know, Dr. Smith is very proud of his doctorate, as well he should be, for it is an accomplishment attained by few. As we also know, most of us address him as Doctor.

Well, several weeks ago I asked him if it was true that he personally visited every classroom in the district at least once a year. He said that it was, indeed, true—all except for Mrs. Wilson's third grade class. I asked him why that was so.

"Mrs. Wilson keeps a pet duck in her class," he told me, "and when she introduced me to the class as Doctor, the damn thing insulted me!"

SPECIAL NOTE: *These are quick, snappy lines that will pull a chuckle from the audience and the subject. Just be certain to suit the lines to the subject for maximum effect.*

122

TOPICS:
Wisdom; keeping one's word; honesty

AUDIENCE:
Adults, particularly good if the subject is well-known
for honesty and truthfulness

As you are aware, we all knew of tonight's event many weeks in advance. I, personally, knew that I would be speaking about our guest of honor, and I really wanted to get to know something about him so that I could present a personal glimpse of him. Consequently, I dropped in to Dr. Smith's office one afternoon and interviewed him for over an hour.

Finally, I asked him what moral principles had guided his life.

"I would say," Dr. Smith told me, "that the two moral qualities on which I have always relied are honesty and wisdom."

"And, how would you define honesty?" I asked.

"Honesty," he answered, "means always keeping your word. Once you have given your word, you never go back on it. If you give your word, that's it!"

"And, what is wisdom?" I asked.

"Wisdom," he said, "is never giving your word on anything!"

SPECIAL NOTE: *Here, again, we must caution you to be circumspect in the use of this story. Before using this, be certain that the subject is someone whose honesty is appreciated by all. We must remember that our goal is to laugh WITH and not AT our subject.*

123

TOPICS:
Job qualifications; doing the job; tests; placement

AUDIENCE:
Suitable for any audience or subject

Recently, Dr. Smith decided that it was time for every worker in the system to be tested. He went out and found a firm that specialized in aptitude tests, and his plan was to have every employee of the district take one of these aptitude tests to see if the employees were suited to the type of work they were doing.

"And," he told his staff, "I am going to set an example. I will take the first test myself!"

True to his word, he did just that and sent it out to be graded by the company.

A week later, Dr. Smith announced that all plans for the aptitude testing had been cancelled.

Shortly thereafter, I saw Dr. Smith and asked him why this had happened.

"Well," he told me, "I really didn't mind when my results came back suggesting that I would do well in an unskilled job, but I did draw the line when they suggested that my best bet was to find work in a business where my father was the boss!"

SPECIAL NOTE: If your school or system has just gone through an extensive testing program, this story is a natural to elicit a great response. Even without that setup, it is funny enough to roast your subject.

124

TOPICS:
Coming home late; married life; quick thinking

AUDIENCE:
Suitable for all audiences and subjects

As I am certain you must be aware, the pressures of Dr. Smith's job are many and varied, and not the least of them has to do with attending meetings that last long into the night. Well, Dr. Smith's wife was becoming rather upset with him for coming in at one, two, and three o'clock in the morning, and she laid down the law. She flatly told him that if he was late just one more time, there was going to be trouble.

One late night shortly thereafter, Dr. Smith came creeping in very quietly in hopes of not disturbing his wife. A floorboard creaked, however, and from upstairs, his wife called, "So you're finally home. What time is it?"

"It's only midnight, my dear," said Dr. Smith. And, at that very moment, the cuckoo clock gave out with three loud cuckoos.

Dr. Smith told me that you have no idea how hard it was for him to stand in the middle of his living room saying, "cuckoo" nine more times!

SPECIAL NOTE: *Use this story only if it is evident to everyone that the subject and his or her spouse are very happily married. This might be adapted for a female subject with no trouble at all.*

Afterthoughts

Throughout this chapter, we have given you stories to use to roast your subject. You should remember, however, that these stories are only a part of your task. Use them to get laughter, but then be certain to shift to some words of positive, heartfelt respect and affection for your subject. Say what is in your heart, and you will never go wrong. Above all, the audience must understand that the roasting you did was all in fun and that you have a sincere affection for the guest.

When you have finished with that and led a round of applause for your subject, it is best to finish on a light note. In that regard, one of our favorite lines is to look at our subject and say, ". . .and now, Dr. Smith, it's up to you. Shall we let these ladies and gentlemen enjoy themselves a little longer, or do you want to make your speech now?"

That never fails to bring another round of laughter and applause, and, while that is going on, you can shake hands with your subject and lead him or her to the microphone.

Part 10
Just Plain Funny

Part 10

Just Plain Funny

T hroughout this book, we have tried to place stories into various categories. The stories in this section, however, will not allow us to do that. These are stories that, although they concern school and family life and the interplay between parent, teacher and child, nevertheless do not fit easily into any of the nine previous categories.

You will, however, find the same uses for them that you did for the others, for they still aim at the heart of the educational scene. These stories are very good for the middle of a speech or to clear the air and establish rapport at all sorts of formal and informal gatherings both in school and out.

So, let's look at some stories that are just plain funny.

125

TOPICS:
Short introductions in various teaching disciplines

AUDIENCE:
Suitable for all adult audiences

I have something very exciting to tell you tonight. You all know Mr. Smith, the chairperson of our Science Department. Well, just a few moments ago, he came to me and told me that he had made a major scientific breakthrough in the school lab.

That's right. He has managed to cross a horse with a black widow spider. He doesn't know what to call the result, but he assures me that if it bites you, you can ride it to the hospital!

* * *

May I present Mrs. Schoeler, who is a long-standing and respected member of our Math Department.

Over the years, Mrs. Schoeler has gained quite a reputation for being able to solve *any* math problem the staff could come up with, and, indeed, many have sought her help with complex mathematical problems at tax time or whenever math was essential to the solution.

She would look at the problem, then take out a small locket *(or medallion, if this is about a gentleman)* she wears around her neck, finger it lovingly, turn away for a moment of silent thought, and turn back with the correct answer.

I always wondered just what was the inspirational secret that locket contained. I fantasized that it was a relic of Sir Isaac Newton or Copernicus or one of the great minds of mathematics that gave Mrs. Schoeler the incentive and inspiration to solve the problem. Then, one day, the chain must have broken, because I found the locket on the floor of her office.

This was my opportunity, and with trembling fingers, I opened it and looked inside. There I found a slip of paper which I opened, and read in hushed silence.

It said, "Two time two equals four; two times three equals six; two times. . ."

* * *

Here we have Ms. Ferron of our Social Studies Department. Mrs. Ferron has made quite a study of American history, and we all regard her as somewhat of an expert.

Just the other day, I asked her if it was really true that George Washington had thrown a dollar across the Potomac River.

"Yes," she answered, "he did. But, it was no big deal."

"No big deal?" I questioned. "That's a very long distance to throw a dollar."

"Sure," she told me, "but in those days, everybody knows that a dollar went a lot further than it does today!"

* * *

Ladies and gentlemen, may I introduce Mr. Haskins of our Physical Education Department. Mr. Haskins also serves as our coach, and was, himself, a fine athlete when he was in school.

In fact, I recently met Mr. Haskins's former football coach, and he told me that during one particularly rough game, he called the young Mr. Haskins to his side.

"Look, Haskins," the coach told him, "I want you to go out there and get belligerent; get vindictive!"

"Sure, Coach," Mr. Haskins replied, "you just give me their numbers, and I'll get those kids right away!"

* * *

And, this is Miss Galtry of our Music Department. Miss Galtry is an accomplished musician and directs our band. She also has a very critical ear for music.

In fact, when she was in college, she wrote for the student newspaper as a music critic. She holds the record, I believe, for the shortest music review on record.

She wrote, "Last night the orchestra played Beethoven. Beethoven lost, 3 to 1."

* * *

Ladies and gentlemen, this is Mr. Bender of our Art Department. Mr. Bender is noted for his work in sculpture and other artistic pursuits. He has served as judge on many occasions for art shows and the like.

He tells me that once he was involved in an exhibit of modern sculpture, and the judges were having a difficult time determining the winner until they came to the very last entry.

It was an old, beat-up tin box from the end of which protruded half of a dill pickle. The judges decided on the spot that this entry exhibited just the spirit, verve, and naturalness for which they were looking. They placed the blue ribbon on it.

Just then, the janitor came running in, snatched the sculpture from the table, and exclaimed, "So there it is! Why can I never remember where I put my lunch!"

*   *   *

And, here, ladies and gentlemen, is Mr. Billings of our English Department. He is, and has been, highly regarded by his students and colleagues for his dedication and his quest for perfection in the English language.

Why, I recall that one graduation the senior class called him up on stage and presented him with a plaque in recognition of his outstanding performance in the teaching of English.

Mr. Billings took the plaque, looked at it, and even from a distance, you could see that tears had sprung to his eyes and were streaming down his cheeks. It was a touching moment. There was, literally, not a dry eye in the place.

Afterward, I went up to Mr. Billings and said, "I could see how touched you were with that plaque, but believe me, you deserve it."

"I wasn't crying because of that!" Mr. Billings answered me. "Of course I deserved it, but those idiots misspelled *recognition!*"

SPECIAL NOTE: *Whether you are hosting a panel discussion, introducing members of your department, or playing master of ceremonies for a program involving the entire faculty, these stories will serve you well. We once attended a Parents Night activity where the entire faculty was introduced using short, humorous anecdotes such as the ones above. It left the audience very well-disposed toward the program which was to follow, and the faculty seemed to enjoy it, too.*

126

TOPICS:
Tedious speeches; activities for parents; principal

AUDIENCE:
Suitable for all adult audiences

It was one of those school activities held in the evening to which the parents of the students are invited. There were a number of speeches, but the speakers all kept their comments short and to the point. All, that is, except the principal of the school who droned on and on, his speech extending from ten minutes to thirty minutes to an hour.

The audience was becoming restless, and there were many grumbles to be heard. Suddenly, there was a loud squeak from the speakers and the public address system went berserk, squealing and squawking.

"What is this?" said the principal from the stage. "If this keeps up, I won't be able to hear myself speak!"

At which point, a loud voice from the rear of the auditorium proclaimed, "Just keep going, mister. Believe me, you ain't missing anything!"

SPECIAL NOTE: If you clear it with him or her first, this would be a humorous way in which to introduce the principal or whoever was assigned to speak. Be sure to ask their permission first, however. We might also ALL take to heart the basic message of this story and keep our own speeches short and to the point.

127

TOPICS:
Modern life; different cultures; questions and answers

AUDIENCE:
Suitable for all adult audiences

The young man approached his father one evening with a problem.

"Dad," he said, "we have to do a research paper for school, and I was wondering if you'd give me your opinion on something."

"Of course, Son," the man replied. "What's your topic?"

"I'm writing about native Americans," replied the boy, "and I'd like to know if you thought that their culture was superior in any way to that of today's society?"

"Was the culture of the American Indian superior to that of today's?" mused the father. "Well, when they were in charge there were no taxes, no credit cards, no unemployment and no inflation— good Lord, my boy, what do you think?"

SPECIAL NOTE: This should get a good laugh from your audience. Remembering the "Good Old Days" is a favorite pastime of many. You might tell this, and then go into an examination of the past, showing how the good old days may not have been so good after all.

128

TOPICS:
Travel; mistaken impressions; misunderstanding

AUDIENCE:
Suitable for all adult audiences

Recently, I had to attend a conference with Mr. Smith, the principal of our school. It was in San Francisco, so we tried to get bookings on an airline. Because we were a little late making our reservations, we couldn't get a direct flight and had to settle for one that made several local stops.

The flight was beautiful, and soon we set down in Pittsburgh where a blue-and-white truck drove out and refueled our plane. Mr. Smith watched the procedure with great interest.

We next touched down in St. Louis where the refueling process again took place thanks to the blue-and-white truck. Again, Mr. Smith watched the proceedings silently.

We were soon off again and landed in Denver where another blue-and-white truck refueled our plane for the final leg.

Finally, we set down in San Francisco, and as we were leaving the plane, another blue-and-white truck was heading out to it.

"Well," I said to Mr. Smith, "we really made good time didn't we?"

"I guess so," answered Mr. Smith, his eyes glued to the field, "but next time let's take that blue-and-white truck. It arrived before we did every single time!"

SPECIAL NOTE: *Of course, it doesn't have to be the principal of the school as in this story. You can make the subject be anyone you wish. Also, be sure to pick a destination and stops along the way that reflect a trip from your area of the country.*

129

TOPICS:

School cafeteria; cafeteria food

AUDIENCE:

Suitable for all audiences including older students

Recently, our principal held a special meeting of the student council in order to seek their suggestions for improving the quality of food in the cafeteria.

He tells me that the best suggestion came from one student who thought that it would be a good idea if the meat was covered in plastic. That way, it would be easier to dust.

* * *

A group of distinguished alumni had returned to the school for a visit, and they were being given a tour through the building by the principal.

"Except for a new coat of paint and a repair here and there," the principal smiled, "you'll find it's the same old place."

As they were going down the stairs, the principal patted the hand railing. "Same old banister," he said.

They entered the cafeteria, and the principal spread his arms and said, "Same old tables."

They went on the food line, and the principal handed them trays. "Yes," he said, "same old trays."

With that, one of the alumni reached over, grabbed a luncheon roll, and tapped it against the counter. It made a loud, clunking sound.

"I see," said the alumnus. "Same old biscuits, too!"

* * *

One young lad came running up to the principal.

"Come quick," he said, "a black cat just got into the cafeteria!"

"I'll get him out," replied the principal, "but you don't have to worry. It's just a superstition that black cats are unlucky."

"Well, this one is sure unlucky!" said the boy. "He just ate a plate of today's surprise special!"

SPECIAL NOTE: Cafeterias and cafeteria workers in our schools usually do a fine job of preparing and serving nutritious food to students under pressing circumstances. It is well to remind your audience of this if you are having a little fun with the cafeteria staff of your school.

130

TOPICS:
Sports; coach; principal

AUDIENCE:
Suitable for all audiences

The local football coach, the chairman of the Physical Education Department, and the principal of the school decided that they would attend an Olympic-like sports event. No one wanted to drive, so they took a train to the location only to find that the stadium was five miles outside of town, and there was no public transportation.

They were standing around bemoaning their fate, when they spotted a large bus which bore the legend *Stadium*. Naturally, they ran toward the vehicle. Upon nearing it, however, they heard the driver talking to a man who had just tried to get on.

"Sorry, buddy," the driver told the man, "but this bus is reserved for the athletes and their equipment. Only the participating athletes can ride."

As they walked away depressed, suddenly the coach raised his head, smiled, and ran into a local department store. He emerged a few moments later with a mop that he had purchased. Quickly, he removed the mop head and, gripping just the mop handle, he approached the bus.

"Jones," he told the driver. "Pole vault!" And, sure enough, the driver let him on the bus.

Suddenly, the department chairman brightened, smiled, and ran around the corner where he pried a hubcap off the first car he came to and ran back to the bus.

"Richards," he said to the bus driver. "Discus throw!" And, the driver let him on the bus as well.

Now, the principal stood alone. Then he, too, brightened and ran into the nearest hardware store.

His two friends were watching from the bus, and they were wondering what the principal was going to come up with. Five minutes passed, then ten. Finally, the two on the bus saw the principal emerge from the hardware store, and even from a distance, they could tell that he was in terrible shape. For one thing, he was limping badly, and for another, it looked as if he were bleeding from numerous places on his body.

As he neared the bus and the driver, they could see that the principal was wrapped from head to toe in barbed wire! The barbed wire not only hindered his movement, but it was cutting into him in several places.

Out of breath and obviously in pain, the principal hobbled up to the bus driver.

"Smith," he panted. "Fencing!"

SPECIAL NOTE: *This story produces a tremendous audience reaction. It is one of the best. We have found it ideal for those "Sports Night" activities or athletic dinners held by most schools. You can then use the name of the team's coach, possibly his assistant, and the principal of the school. It doesn't matter if these people are men or women, the story can be told about them. Remember to have the one you wish to roast in the final position. If the coach is to be honored in some way, it is good to have the joke on him or her. Try this one, and you'll love the reaction.*

131

TOPICS:
Snappy answers; parents and children; the age-old
battle of raising kids

AUDIENCE:
Suitable for all adult audiences, particularly parents

After their twelve-year-old daughter had retired for the night,
the wife interrupted her husband as he sat reading his newspaper.

"Honey," she said to him, "today I had a very frank discussion
with our daughter concerning the facts of life."

"Really," said the father leaning forward and whispering in a
conspiratorial tone. "What did you learn?"

*   *   *

Twelve-year-old Bob had just brought home his report card, and
his father "hit the roof"!

"What is the meaning of this?" the father exclaimed. "Why, do
you realize that when George Washington was your age he had
already become a surveyor and was out working and earning a living!"

"Yeah," young Bob mumbled under his breath, "and when he
was your age he was president!"

*   *   *

Father wanted his son to become a lawyer, so ever since the lad
could understand, his father had told him stories about what lawyers
did and filled him with tales of Clarence Darrow and Abe Lincoln as
lawyers. This work seemed to pay off, for the boy soon began reading
biographies and novels about lawyers and finally began to look into
case histories. Father was delighted.

One day, however, Father came into the living room to find his
son reading a book titled, *Proper Methods of Raising Your Child.*

"Well, Son," laughed Father, "are you learning how to become
a parent?"

"Oh, no," said the boy, "I'm just checking to see if you and Mother brought me up properly. I think I may have grounds for a suit!"

* * *

"Gosh, Pop," said the young boy as he finished mowing the law, "when do I get to be old enough to do only what *I* want to do?"

"Nobody knows, Son," answered the lad's father. "No one has ever lived that long yet!"

* * *

"What's the matter, Son?" asked Father. "You look a little sad."

"It's nothing important, Dad," said the youngster. "It's just that I was bothered by arthritis in school today."

Father's mouth dropped open, and he immediately bundled the boy off to the family doctor who thoroughly examined the lad and pronounced him in fine health. He definitely did *not*, the doctor told his father, have arthritis.

"Son," said the father, "I don't understand. You told me that today you were bothered in school by arthritis."

"I sure was, Dad!" exclaimed the boy. "The teacher asked me how to spell it twice, and I couldn't!"

SPECIAL NOTE: *Again, these are the short, to-the-point, stories that may be used in the body of various speaking assignments.*

132

TOPICS:

Table manners; embarrassment; unexpected guests; family

AUDIENCE:

Suitable for all audiences, particularly parents

Mother took little Billy aside and told him, "Billy, I made a terrible mistake with the dessert for tonight's dinner when your Aunt Mary and Uncle Joe are over. I made too little, and there isn't enough to go around. So, I'm going to ask a favor of you. When it comes time for dessert, just say that you don't want any. That way, there will be enough to go around. For a reward, tomorrow I'll buy you the biggest ice cream soda you want."

Billy quickly agreed, and that night at the dinner table, when his mother asked him if he wanted dessert, he politely refused.

"Oh, come now, Billy," said Aunt Mary, "surely you can handle some dessert."

"No, thank you, Aunt Mary."

"Come on, Bill," Uncle Joe enjoined, "I've never seen you miss dessert before."

"No, thank you, Uncle Joe."

"Really, Billy," Aunt Mary pressed, "you must have some of this . . ."

"Look!" Billy interrupted, "You don't know the terrible mistake Mom made when she made that dessert, so just leave me alone, and I'll have a decent dessert later!"

*   *   *

Aunt Mary had some deep concerns about the way her niece was raising little Tommy, but she really didn't feel that she should interfere. On one visit to Aunt Mary's home, however, young Tommy became so obstreperous, that Aunt Mary figured she had to say something. She decided to approach the subject obliquely.

"Alice," she said to her niece, "isn't it terrible how some parents nowadays just let their children do whatever they want without any discipline? You know what I mean, dear. Some children don't listen when they are spoken to, they throw temper tantrums, they. . ." And, Aunt Mary went on for several moments describing a typical "spoiled" child which, she conceived, young Tommy certainly was.

When Aunt Mary had stopped, Tommy's mother looked at her with a faint smile and said, "Thank you, Aunt Mary. Thank you for being so polite."

Aha, thought Aunt Mary, it has finally sunk in, and now she wants to thank me for being so gentle with her.

"Why, Alice," said Aunt Mary, "whatever do you mean by that?"

"Well," said Tommy's mother, "when you were going on about those terrible children, I recognized every other youngster on the block, but I notice that you never once described Tommy, and I thought that was very polite of you!"

SPECIAL NOTE: *Manners vary from individual to individual, and mis-understandings, both the comic and the not-so-comic, can and often do occur. These stories offer both aspects of the subject, and they are all very well received.*

Afterthoughts

Rest assured that you will find ample opportunity to use the stories in this chapter. Not only are they funny enough to elicit laughter, but they may often be used to prove a point, start a discussion, or make people think about a variety of subjects.

Remember, everybody likes to laugh, and if you can start them laughing, you have their attention and good will. This is a great beginning to any relationship.

A Final Word

Years ago, we came upon a poem which we give to you now. Memorize it and keep it with you at all times. Let it teach you the wonder and the power of joy.

> *Laugh, and the world laughs with you;*
> *Weep, and you weep alone;*
> *For the sad old earth must borrow its mirth,*
> *But has trouble enough of its own.*
> *—Ella Wheeler Wilcox*

May the gift of laughter be yours—now and throughout all your tomorrows.

TOPIC
FINDER

HOW TO USE THIS TOPIC FINDER

This section makes it possible for you to quickly locate the correct anecdote or story for the topic you have in mind. It is thoroughly and vigorously cross-indexed, and it can direct you to exactly the material you require in a matter of seconds.

The numbers following the topics in this index indicate the numbers of the anecdotes or stories in which the topic is covered. They are not page numbers. Look up your topic, and you will immediately be directed to the anecdotes or stories that contain information on it.

Look for the larger topic first, and see what you can find. Then, you may wish to look up some of the topics which you would consider as subheadings of your major topic.

For example, suppose you wanted an anecdote or story about the principal of the school. First, look up "principal," and you will be given a number of stories that apply. But, you might also want to look up "Superintendent of Schools" and incorporate some of the material under the various subheadings such as "and principals," et cetera. In this way, you will find considerable supplementary material.

Whatever your intent, this TOPIC FINDER will prove invaluable.

Index